Tom Morris shares his vision for his clients with his readers; to provide the simplest and most effective assistance with the least amount of effort. Thank you for such an understandable book.

Sharon Armstrong, Author
Stress-free Performance Appraisals
Turn Your Most Painful Management Duty Into
A Powerful Motivational Tool

Tom has helped thousands of our clients through tough transitions and his articles reflect his seasoned career.

William B. Owen, Ph.D., Deputy Director
US Department of State

Tom Morris, a career consultant and speaker, provides strategies and advice grounded in over 25 years of work in the field; I especially appreciate his writing on presentations.

Lynne Waymon, Co – author
Make Your Contact Counts

Tom is a very rare professional who has the ability to work with all levels of employees from executives down to semi-skilled hourly paid workers, with equal effectiveness.

Richard Paris, Vice President of Human Resources
Roswell Park Cancer Institute

Tom provides detailed and practical advice for all those involved in recruiting, selecting, and retaining employees in today's economy.

John P. Hannah, President and CEO
Leadercoach, LLC

Tom Morris has a breadth of knowledge and expert advice for the Human Resources director. This innovative book hits a number of common and difficult issues right on target. Take notes!

Michele Fantt-Harris, Director of Human Resources
The National Cooperative Bank

A book that provides real answer to real questions, I was particularly impressed by his insights for human resources professionals.

Linda S. Aitken, Director, Human Resources & Services
American Insurance Association

CAREER MECHANICS I

Solutions to Common Career and Employment Issues

ADVICE ON:

Career Development,
Recruitment and Retention,
Changing Jobs, Career Assessment, Resumes,
Networking, Interviewing and Negotiation

Thomas W. Morris III, CMF

CAREER MECHANICS I
Solutions to Common Career and Employment Issues

Thomas W. Morris III, CMF

All rights reserved. No part of this book may be reproduced or transmitted in any form or by any means, electronic or mechanical, including photocopying, recording or otherwise, without written permission from the author.

Copyright © 2006, by Morris Associates, Inc. All rights reserved.
Printed in the United States of America.

Published by Tal San Publishing — Bramor Distributing

Bramor Distributing
1717 K Street, NW, Suite 1200
Washington, DC 20036

Some of the material in this book appeared in earlier versions in essays by the author which appeared in publications including *Executive Update, Careerbuilder.com, Capital Connection, RCJobs.com, Realtors, Washington Business Journal, Career Planning and Adult Development Journal, and Washingtonjobs.com* .

Catalogue-in-Publication Data Added by Author

Morris III, Thomas W.
    CAREER MECHANICS I: Solutions to Common Career
        and Employment Issues
      1. Career Development 2. Recruitment and Retention
      3. Changing Jobs   4. Career Assessment   5. Resumes
        6. Networking   7. Interviewing   8. Negotiation.
Includes précis, endnotes and index.

ISBN 1-884298-74-5

Library of Congress Control Number: 2005937535

Printed in the United States by Morris Publishing, Kearney, NE

To my mom, Alice Anna Morris, who showed me how to have courage and appreciate life's blessings,

and to my dad, Thomas Weber Morris, from whom I got my name and learned to be a gentle man.

Table of Contents

Précis   4

Acknowledgments   13

Introduction   15

Section I - Guidance for Career Seekers

Attitude

Developing a Positive Attitude	19
Image and Success: What Do We Base Our First Impressions On?	22
Vision	24
Look Where You Want to Go: Lessons from the Racetrack	26

Assessment

Looking for a New Direction?	28
When It's Time to Go, It's Time to Go	31
When the Career Ladder Appears Horizontal	33

Resumes

Choosing an Effective Resume Format	35
Creating a Future-Directed Resume	40
Resumes: Stating Objectives and Capitalizing on Gaps in Employment	43

Career Change Process/Special Situations

Singing the Too-Qualified Blues	46
Establishing Credibility Without a College Degree	48
Transitioning Out of Human Resources: Many Options	50
Transitioning from the Federal Government to the Private Sector	53
Should I Stay or Should I Go?	57
Why December May Be the Best Month for a Job Search	59
Company Layoffs: Surviving and Thriving	61

Networking, Interviewing and Negotiating

Networking and Interviewing	64
Finding a Job by Associating with Associations	71
Dances with Interviews	74
The Etiquette of References	77
The ABC's of Executive Compensation	80
Interviews and Offers	84

SECTION II - GUIDANCE FOR EMPLOYEES

In the Workplace

Communicating with Difficult Bosses or Supervisors	88
Profiling a Great Boss	92
Too Close for Comfort: The Limits on Workplace Relationships	94
Sexual Harassment Claims and Retaliation	97
Changing a Light Bulb	100
Career Insurance	102
The Effects of Technology	106

SECTION III - GUIDANCE FOR HUMAN RESOURCES MANAGERS

Recruiting and Retention

Designing Your Interviews to Select Good Employees	110
Acquainting New Employees with Your Organization's Core Values	115
When a New Hire Doesn't Measure Up	118
Employment of People with Disabilities	121
The ABC's of Relationships	124
Retaining Valued Employees in a Competitive Environment	127

Layoffs and Reductions in Force

Alternatives to Downsizing	131
Managing a Downsizing	134

SECTION IV - GUIDANCE FOR CAREER COACHES

Career Assessment: Many Approaches	140
Advice from Successful Job Seekers	143
How to Avoid Being De-selected	145
Career Management and Quality of Life	149
A Workshop on the Employment of People with Disabilities	152

CLOSING

Endnotes	159
Index	160
About the Author	166
Contact Us	167

PRÉCIS

SECTION I - GUIDANCE FOR CAREER SEEKERS

ATTITUDE

Developing a Positive Attitude

The most important predictor of a successful transition is a positive mental attitude. Here is guidance on how to use positive self-talk to help you realize your career goals.

Image and Success: What Do We Base Our First Impressions On?

Look your best! First impressions are based on presence, facial expressions and communication style.

Vision

Using self-talk and self-thought to increase the probability that your future will be prosperous.

Look Where You Want To Go: Lessons from the Racetrack

High performance drivers and successful career changers share a trait: they look ahead and stay positive. Take your job search to the racetrack and master sharp turns and interviews.

Assessment

Looking for a New Direction?

Help build your future by understanding your style, attitude and past. Try these two exceptional assessment exercises, *Factoring Your Past Accomplishments* and *Cloning Yourself*.

When It's Time to Go, It's Time to Go

If you are unsatisfied with your current job, it may be time to move on.

When the Career Ladder Appears Horizontal

Facing a career transition? As you face tough decisions, make sure you are asking the right questions.

Resumes

Choosing an Effective Resume Format

Will your resume pass the "quick-glance test?" Strengthen your resume with an appropriate format.

Creating the Future-Directed Resume

Most resumes are obituaries. They explain what you have already done. What you need now is a future-directed resume that outlines what you are able to do for someone else.

Resumes: Stating Objectives and Capitalizing on Gaps in Employment

Learn to explain your experiences in a positive light. Check out these simple resume hints for presenting the best possible picture of yourself.

Career Change Process / Special Situations

Singing the Too-Qualified Blues

The real factors in whether you are selected for a job are your attitude, aptitude and fit with the hiring organization.

Establishing Credibility Without a College Degree

Create a resume that highlights your experience and professional traits. Accentuate any relevant training and education you have had, and show employers why you are the best fit for the position.

Transitioning Out of Human Resources: Many Options

Many skills overlap and are transferable between different positions and businesses.

Transitioning from the Federal Government to the Private Sector

You can relate the skills of your current job to the qualifications for your next. Focusing on your strengths can help you win employment in a new field.

Should I Stay or Should I Go?

Don't stay in a job you hate. If you can't move aside, move on.

Why December May Be the Best Month for a Job Search

When is the best time to search for a job? The answer may surprise you.

Company Layoffs: Surviving and Thriving

Should you expect a layoff in your organization? Here are some clues and an outline of the steps you can take to strengthen your position and make your work more valuable to your employer.

Networking, Interviewing and Negotiating

Networking and Interviewing

The best way to search for a job is to seek information and to build a network of professionals in the industry of your interest. Learn what questions to ask, how to prepare your resume, and how to interview effectively.

Finding a Job by Associating with Associations

Associations present a great source of fast exposure and information on fields of interest to career changers and job seekers. See how to find and benefit from associations and trade groups.

Dances with Interviews

How to handle phone and group interviews, and how to conduct them properly.

The Etiquette of References

A simple guide for asking for references and learning what to do in sticky reference situations.

The ABC's of Executive Compensation

Practical advice on how to know and negotiate your worth in the marketplace.

Interviews and Offers

What questions should you ask when faced with multiple job offers? Look at the whole picture. Create a framework to help you make the right decision.

Section II - Guidance for Employees

In the Workplace

Communicating with Difficult Bosses or Supervisors

Learn how to avoid a potentially bad relationship with a boss. Remember, you are ultimately responsible for your own career.

Profiling a Great Boss

Bosses are generally appreciated by their employees. Discover what qualities employees appreciate in a great boss.

Too Close for Comfort: The Limits of Workplace Relationships

This article offers advice on how to build and maintain healthy relationships at work.

Sexual Harassment Claims and Retaliation

Learn how to recognize harassment and handle complaints and retaliation.

Changing a Light Bulb

Tom's planning rule: whatever you plan, it'll take twice as long and cost three times as much.

Career Insurance

This article provides a number of excellent resolutions you could make to enhance your career. By initiating each resolution with a positive attitude, you will be more likely to reach your career goals.

The Effects of Technology

Technology has changed the way companies manage support staff and clerical tasks. How does that affect the role and job description of a professional?

Section III - Guidance for Human Resources Managers

Recruiting and Retention

Designing Your Interviews to Select Good Employees

Learn how to develop a strategy for interviewing job candidates to find the best possible for the positions you need to fill.

Acquainting New Employees with Your Organization's Core Values

An organization's mission is expressed in the attitude of each employee. Discover ways to assure that your employees are kept mindful of your values.

When a New Hire Doesn't Measure Up

How do you deal with new hires who don't perform as you thought they would? This essay contains advice on what to do with an employee who is not meeting your expectations.

Employment of People with Disabilities

How can a company successfully incorporate people with disabilities into its workforce?

The ABC's of Relationships

What is the key to a great relationship? Have a look at the elements of excellent workplace relationships.

Retaining Valued Employees in a Competitive Environment

In today's competitive market, workplaces need to create a culture of respect, challenge and rewards. Acquire tactics for keeping your talented employees.

LAYOFFS AND REDUCTIONS IN FORCE

Alternatives to Downsizing

Preserve morale and productivity. Prepare a plan that will help your organization sidestep the possible repercussions of large downsizings.

Managing a Downsizing

If you determine that a downsizing is unavoidable, read these suggestions on how to make the transition smoother.

SECTION IV - GUIDANCE FOR CAREER COACHES

Career Assessment: Many Approaches

Helping someone find his or her dream job may necessitate identifying the job-seeker's dream. These exercises can help.

Advice from Successful Job Seekers

Integrate these tried-and-true components into the job–search process, and help job seekers conduct more effective searches.

How to Avoid Being De-selected

By knowing what *not* to do in a job search, a person can improve his or her chances in a competitive job market. These suggestions encompass all aspects of the job search: attitude, resumes, interviewing and follow-up.

Career Management and Quality of Life

Trends in the field of career management have been changing. Stay abreast of the new paths.

A Workshop on the Employment of People with Disabilities

Learn strategies to help guide people with disabilities as they make career transitions.

*This book is a way to give back something of
what I have learned from and experienced with others.*

TWM III

ACKNOWLEDGMENTS

When I reflect on the project of writing, editing and producing this book (and another which is soon to be published), I am amazed at the number of people who helped me translate my ideas into reality. (It makes me better appreciate why there are so many people named in the credits at the end of movies.) Some of the credit belongs to people who helped shape the text; some belongs to those who helped shape the author. It is a pleasure to salute each of them:

> Amy Hammond, for laying out and proofreading the text, compiling the index, and managing the project; and Tom O'Herron, for his careful editing, advice and encouragement.
>
> Mary Taylor, for assembling materials for the book, and for managing the first part of the entire project.
>
> Morgan Hanners, for the benefit of his experience in assembling material and organizing the project.
>
> Sandi Lloyd of Tal San Publishing, who guided us through the printing, production and sometimes mysterious ways of transferring digital information to printed words.

Warm thanks also to those who contributed substantive ideas and editorial suggestions: Linda Aitken, Sharon Armstrong, Monica Arredondo, Dennis Austin, Linda Barker, T.C. Benson, Gisele Cloutier, Mike DeBruhl, Armand De Filippo, Mark Gonska, Elaine Gregg, John Hannah, Michele Fantt Harris, Christopher Harrison, Nedra Hartzell, Jo Ellen Huffer, Amy Joyce, Anne Kontner, Joan Marshall, Emory Mulling, Carlos Munoz, Keith Nave, Bill Owen, Rick Parris, Alan Pickman, Mike Reddy, Elliot Rosen, Gordon Rowe, Dr. Robert Rudney, Jane Salemen, Susan Sarfati, Jane Schultz, Nan Siemer, Gordon Silcox, Larry Stybel, Jane Trevaskis and Lynne Waymon.

In addition to recognizing their professional work, I want to acknowledge the personal support of Seth Sandler, Becca Ford, Morgan Hanners, Mary Taylor, Amy Hammond and Tom O'Herron. Their friendship, laughter and loyalty have made it possible for us to manage a successful business while putting together two books as neophytes in the publishing world. Each of them gets a star!

Among those who shaped my ideas and love of books, I want to acknowledge my grandmother, parents, aunts and uncles, who often took time to read to me and helped me become a reader at very young age.

Throughout my school years I was fortunate to have many fine teachers. I owe special thanks to Sisters Elizabeth and Patricia Mary at Bayley-Ellard High School, Madison, New Jersey, who advised, "If you want impact in your writing, do it with your copy, not your punctuation." I follow that advice to this day.

At Boston University's Graduate School of Public Communications, Professor William Sullivan showed me how to edit to improve readability. I still remember and apply his teachings about active verbs, the use of personal references, dynamic and mechanical flow, sentence length and variation.

I also want to recognize the help given by many of my colleagues in the National Speakers Association, especially Doug Smart, Arnold Sanow and Dan Poynter.

Finally, I would like to thank Jann Bradley, my wife, business partner and best friend, for her creative support and unfailing encouragement. I am indeed blessed to have her as my partner in life and work.

INTRODUCTION

In this book we look at the hiring and supervision process from *both sides* of the employment table. The essays which follow are addressed to several related audiences: job seekers, career changers, and employees seeking to move up; and personnel managers, workplace supervisors, and career coaches. These groups have overlapping interests, so that material primarily designed for, say, job seekers will likely be helpful to career coaches (and others) as well.

Fortunately, there seems to be no shortage of women and men who have the resilience, willpower and daring to move beyond obstacles and setbacks so as to reach and embrace more interesting ways to earn their livings. The great satisfaction of my work has been to help many such people channel their imaginations, energies and efforts effectively so that they find and enjoy the right jobs.

It is my hope that this book will do the same for you.

TWM

Disclaimer

The author of this book is not engaged in giving legal advice. If the reader requires legal assistance, he/she should seek the counsel of a competent attorney.

The information in this book is meant to complement other information available to readers about the subjects discussed.

Although many people made contributions and gave advice for this book, the final copy and opinions are the author's, and he takes responsibility for them.

The author of this book shall have neither liability nor responsibility to any person or entity with respect to any loss or damage caused or alleged to be caused directly or indirectly by reliance upon information in this book.

SECTION I

Guidance for Career Seekers

*"Make it something you want to do,
not something you have to do."*

-Alice Anna Morris

ATTITUDE

Developing a Positive Attitude

My 25 years as a career counselor have taught me that the most reliable predictor of an individual's successful career transition is not a great resume or a distinguished educational background, but rather a *positive mental attitude*. Whether a person chooses to change careers, or changes because of external circumstances, a successful transition depends on the ability to develop and maintain a positive mental attitude.

In his book, *Joe DiMaggio: The Promise*, Joe Carrieri, a former New York Yankees' batboy, recounts the positive mental attitude that led to the renowned Yankee hitter's success.[i] "He didn't *think* they would win, he didn't *believe* that they would win, he *knew* that they would win. His very presence in the lineup changed the balance of power between the Yankees and their opponents."

In fact, athletic trainers and coaches have known for years that the key to creating a champion athlete is cultivating the athlete's ability to visualize success. Sports psychologists have outlined a program for creating a positive mental attitude; it can be applied to all career professionals.

When faced with losing a job or some other negative career change, negative emotions kick in, and often give rise to irrational judgments like "I've failed," or "I'm no good," or "Nobody wants someone my age."

When these judgments are expressed aloud, the brain registers them as "truths," and the "truths" often give rise to further negative reactions, which can be sensed by others. Negative self-talk builds negative self-image, which in turn can influence performance. *Negative visualizations foster poor performance.*

POSITIVE MENTAL ATTITUDE

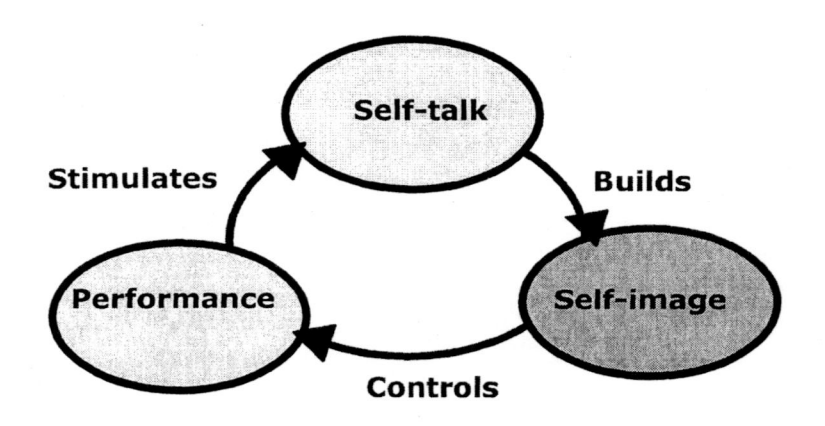

```
        Self-talk
   Stimulates    Builds
Performance      Self-image
        Controls
```

This is understandable; it is natural for our emotions to influence our actions. In fact, the word "emotion" comes from the Latin prefix *e*, meaning "out of," and the Latin verb *movēre*, meaning "to move."[ii]

Emotional reactions to life crises like divorce, illness, death of a loved one, or the loss of a job generally follow the same pattern of negative feelings regarding undesired (and often unanticipated) change. However, once we recognize this pattern as a natural process, it becomes much easier to fast-forward through the negative stages and quickly transition to a positive attitude and positive behavior.

But direct effort to change emotions doesn't usually work very well; it's better to try to balance the emotions with reason.

As the Greek philosopher Epictetus wrote 2,000 years ago, "Only you can upset yourself about events. The events themselves, no matter how undesirable, can never upset you."

So in the face of disappointment we need to ask rational questions like:

- ➢ What have I succeeded at in life?
- ➢ Is it true that no one my age ever gets employed?
- ➢ What am I good at?

Once these questions are answered rationally (which is to say, realistically), positive self-talk can follow, and that in turn can create positive visualizations, which can lead to the realization of one's career (or other) goals.

To sum up: creating a positive mental image of yourself and your accomplishments automatically reduces the natural anxiety caused by disappointment, and is an effective step toward positive outcomes.

Image and Success: What Do We Base Our First Impressions On?

The word "image" suggests that what is represented is not the real thing. The term carries a negative connotation. It is commonly perceived that your "image" is not the real "you."

"Image," according to *Webster's New Collegiate Dictionary*, is "the concept of someone or something that is held by the public," or "the character projected by someone or something that is a mental picture of something not real or present."[iii]

Assuming you have developed character traits associated with success, how do you project the corresponding image? Useful techniques can be roughly divided into three areas: how you dress, how you speak and listen to others, and how you maintain a positive mental attitude. All of these can be learned, and then improved with practice. For starters, here are three guidelines that can help almost anyone convey the image of success.

First, look presentable. Have your clothes pressed, shirt or blouse neatly laundered, and shoes shined. The biggest single mistake a professional can make in dressing is to look sloppy and uncaring about his or her appearance. If you're uncertain in this regard, you might ask an acquaintance and someone you don't know well for their reactions to your appearance.

Second, dress with the receiver's reactions in mind. Remember, when you meet someone, you are not merely projecting an image, someone else is receiving one, too.

Third, when selecting your clothes for an interview, dress conservatively while maintaining your individuality.

Beyond dress, the most important element of image is the face. We are identified by facial characteristics, and we communicate with others through speech and facial expressions.

The vast majority of an emotional message is communicated non-verbally. Your face can convey the positive character traits you wish to project. In the long run, most people can sense when others are genuine or when they are being insincere.

Eye contact is probably the single most important indicator of our non-verbal messages. Too little eye contact may lead others to think that you are not listening to them. Too much can be perceived as staring. That can project an overbearing personality, making other people anxious.

After the eyes, the mouth is most important. The tone of your voice and smile can go a long way in making people feel comfortable, and even important. Practice smiling into the mirror in the morning and into the telephone when you talk. Smile when you meet people, to reassure them that you are friendly and approachable.

Finally, listen. More precisely, listen and learn. Listen to words; listen for needs. And tune in to the non-verbal messages of those with whom you converse. Avoid interrupting someone who is speaking.

In summary, key behaviors to think about when you are consciously trying to improve your image are how you dress, how you smile, how you talk to people and how you listen to people.

Character + Positive Mental Attitude + Open Communication = Positive Image.

Vision

Our vision, both ocular and mental, matters. What we focus on, and how we see it, makes a difference in how we react — what we do and how we do it. If you're focusing your sights on the negative, then you will likely react defensively and without creative imagination. But if you look at the positive side of whatever you are facing, you are much more likely to be able to turn a tough situation into an opportunity.

The field of sports gives us many good examples of the power of a positive mental attitude.

For centuries, coaches and trainers of world-class athletes have studied what makes a champion. They wonder, as we do, what separates a gold medal winner from a silver or bronze medal winner. Many experts insist that most often, the key difference isn't speed, strength or fitness: the crucial difference is that a top winner has a healthy inner vision and a strong, positive mental attitude.

This principle also applies to individuals and organizations. A typical manager of an organization focused on downsizing might well not have a plan for recovery, but a forward-looking manager will create a detailed plan for how to handle the aftermath of his organization's downsizing.

A few years ago, the president of a company that underwent a downsizing prepared, in advance, a concise and informative plan for the smaller workforce. Immediately after notices of layoffs were given, he and other key executives met with the remaining staff. After letting people know what had happened that morning, he posted financial goals for the reduced staff.

"I can't guarantee we won't have another downsizing, but this is what we need to do to avoid one," he told his staff. "We need you to help us make these numbers and then we'll be able to move forward together."

The people in the firm rallied and pulled together. In the end, they exceeded their performance objectives.

I've seen similar results over the years. Particularly gratifying are the cases of individuals who made the leap from successful, well-paying careers to follow their dreams — the paths of their lifetime goals. An accountant took advantage of a corporate downsizing by becoming a successful franchise owner. A young White House speechwriter, who lost his job when a new administration came to power, turned down several promising full-time job opportunities to work as a part-time writer so he could prepare for and compete in an Iron Man Triathlon. Both succeeded because they saw clearly what they wanted and concentrated on the road ahead, not on the problem at hand. All job seekers should do the same.

Look Where You Want to Go: Lessons from the Racetrack

Vic Elford, a world-class Team Porsche driver and winner of races at Daytona, Sebring, Monte Carlo and Norburgring, wrote in his book *Porsche High-Performance Driving Handbook*, to:

> Be aware of what is happening all around you: to the sides, using your peripheral vision; to the rear, using your mirrors; and especially way ahead in front of you. Try to look through the windows in the car in front to see what is happening down the road. If that is not possible, drop back a little so that you can see past one side or the other, particularly if the road bends a little.[iv]

As a life-long learner, you continually encounter ways to enhance your understanding of things you already know. I was reminded of that recently when I had the chance to chat with a business writer from *The Washington Post*. We were discussing how to guide organizations through change, especially downsizings, which in government circles are generally called "reductions in force," or RIF's. Specifically, we were discussing factors that managers need to focus on when planning, implementing and recovering from a downsizing.

"It's like being on an auto racetrack," I said. "One of the key things you learn at the track and at all the major driving schools is ocular driving: 'Look where you want to go.' It's the same with management and careers."

"What do you mean?" she asked.

"If you go into a skid," I asked, "what's the first thing you should do?"

"Hit the brakes?" she asked.

I said, "Look where you want the car to go."

The lessons learned driving cars on a track may be applied to managing an organization or navigating through life, especially when times are tough or when you make a mistake. Some people go into a skid, grip the wheel until their knuckles are white, look directly at the object they most want to avoid hitting, and then scream, "Oh my gosh, I'm going to hit that!" Then they usually do.

The internationally known BSR high performance and security driving school of West Virginia instructs its students, "Look where you want to go. Drivers under stress focus on a negative goal, what they think they will hit . . . since you steer where you look, always focus on a positive goal."

Similarly, Bob Bondurant wrote in his book, *Bob Bondurant on High Performance Driving*, "Look ahead. Don't drive off the nose of your car.[v] Focus on what is happening ahead so you have plenty of time to make necessary corrections to the car if there is an emergency. If there is a turn coming up, you have proper time to read how to enter it."

With your career, always look ahead, focus on what is happening around you and plan for an emergency, such as a downsizing, so that you can take care of yourself and move forward. Steer toward a positive direction, give yourself time to correct your career course and stay focused on your goal, not the obstacles in your path.

ASSESSMENT

Looking for a New Direction?

There are two self-assessment exercises which are particularly helpful to individuals who are thinking about career change. They may be called *Factoring Your Past Accomplishments*, and *Cloning Yourself*. In the course of my career, I've done both exercises several times to redefine who I am, what I value, how I want to be and what I want to accomplish.

The first exercise, *Factoring Your Past Accomplishments*, I credit to Dr. Bernard Haldane. Dr. Haldane worked with the US military during World War II to help decide where to place thousands of inductees. After the war, he applied his knowledge and techniques to help returning veterans choose careers.

Start the *Factoring Accomplishments* exercise by listing 12 to 15 events in your life that may have been difficult or uncomfortable, but that you did well, enjoyed doing or were proud of. Include events from both your personal and your professional life. Then rank them in order of importance. Analyze what you see.

Select the most significant eight or ten from this list. Reflect on each event and write down the steps you took, the skills you used and the personal traits you displayed during each event. Repeat this process for accomplishments or events that were not particularly difficult or uncomfortable. At this point you will begin to see patterns and be able to determine the directions and approaches that are best for you.

I saw gratifying results from the second exercise, *Cloning Yourself*, in a career assessment workshop which a colleague and I conducted for EXCEL! Networking Group, Inc., a self-help group of professionals with disabilities. The exercise leaps over limitations, and allows the participants to have their "clones" do or be whatever they wish. With EXCEL!, the participants successfully expressed who they would be if they were liberated from their disabilities.

In the cloning exercise, you are assessing your fantasies and goals. First, set aside practical considerations, such as financial constraints and physical handicaps. Then list the careers, jobs or activities you would pursue if you could clone yourself into five different people and have them do or be *anything at all*.

Let yourself go! Resist self-censorship, and stifle that little voice that says, "This is not possible!" Next to the activity chosen for each clone, explain in writing why you chose that particular activity for that particular clone, and mention the skills you have that would help you carry on the activity.

There are several things I like about these two exercises. First, the exercises help us look at our lives from two different views: one looks backward and inward, the other has a forward and outward perspective. Second, both exercises ask us to reflect on positives: successes, goals achieved, satisfaction, ideals and motivation.

Successful people have positive mental attitudes. Research and experience show that a positive attitude starts with self-talk and inner visions of success. "Stinkin' thinkin,'" as speaker and author Stephen Covey calls it, can be a career- and satisfaction-killer.[vi]

Finally, I like both exercises because they produce lists of skills you can cross-check and rank. This information, coupled with the thought, reflection and focus that both exercises require, will prepare you to compose a future-directed resume, and to make sound decisions about your career and your life.

When It's Time to Go, It's Time to Go

A woman who signed herself "Restless" wrote to me a few years ago to say that after three years with the same trade association and some fairly decent salary increases, she was bored stiff. She loved the industry her association represented, and she was intrigued by the cutting-edge work that some of the association's member firms were doing, but she had concluded that her job responsibilities were not going to grow.

"Restless" had been approached by member firms of her association about going to work for them, and she wondered if she didn't owe it to herself to look at such opportunities. But she also felt at home in the environment of her non-profit association, and was unsure if she would be as comfortable in a for-profit enterprise.

I strongly encouraged "Restless" to consider other options. She had admitted being bored, and that her job responsibilities weren't going to grow. Her high regard for the industry she represented, and her interest in the cutting-edge work being done by some of the companies in that field, did not seem to me to outweigh the dissatisfaction of her current position and its limited future.

If you are approached by a potential employer, your response should not be, "No thank you, I'm happy where I am," since that would close the door on opportunities which might be of great interest. Whether you are ready to change jobs or not, you should always be building a professional network. Reply to a "feeler" with, "Let's talk," or "What do you have in mind? What do you need?"

I don't think it's useful to try to determine whether it would be better for someone to work for a non-profit or for-profit enterprise. I have worked and managed in both. I don't believe that anyone can make a universally applicable statement about the general nature of either type of organization.

The key is to determine the kind of people you want to work with, the kind of work you want to do, and the kind of environment in which you will be challenged, productive and satisfied. You may find the right mix in many non-profit or for-profit organizations.

Years ago, when I was leaving a non-profit, community-based organization, I was trying to sort out what I wanted to do next. I knew it would be something that involved working with and helping people, and my thinking was focused on continuing to work with community-based non-profits.

Over lunch with a colleague, I described the kind of work I wanted to do and expressed some frustration that my preferences virtually assured that I would have to continue working in non-profit associations.

He urged me to broaden my horizons, stating confidently, "Tom, you can work in any kind of organization or business and still do good for people." He was right, of course, as I have seen over and over again in recent years.

"Restless," my correspondent mentioned above, seemed pretty clear as to where she wanted to go professionally. It seemed to me, and I told her, that she should consider the adage, "When it's time to go, it's time to go."

When the Career Ladder Appears Horizontal

Many people wonder whether career moves, to be successful, have to be *up*, rather than sideways. Take the case of one executive who has ten years of experience with medium and large trade associations. The executive was recently offered a senior staff position with an association where she would do roughly the same things she is doing now, but with additional staff to supervise, and a larger budget to manage.

She was having a difficult time determining if the change would be a lateral move, not in the right direction, which she said was *up*.

Most people who change jobs do roughly the same thing(s) they did before. The nature of the work is only *one* basis for comparing a current job with another. There are many other very important factors to be weighed.

If you have a choice between two similar jobs, here are some of the important questions to consider:

- Where are you going? Where do you want to go? How will you get there? What is your plan?
- Which position provides more opportunity for the future?
- Which boss, board and team of coworkers are more compatible with you?
- Which job pays better?
- How do benefits compare? What benefits are most important to you?
- How do travel and commuting requirements compare?
- What is the potential for advancement in each position?

- What will you learn in the new position? Whom will you meet?
- What are your other options?
- What will be the effect of each position on your personal time and your lifestyle?
- How much time will commuting take?

Some people resist lateral moves because *the titles of the old and new positions are the same.* If that's a sticking point for you, why not see if you can negotiate for additional duties and responsibilities *and* a more prestigious title?

Resumes

Choosing an Effective Resume Format

After you have completed a career assessment, and when you have written a strong opening statement with a future-directed perspective, you are ready to write the rest of your resume.

Most books and articles suggest three possible formats for a resume: reverse chronological, functional, or functional and chronological combination. Practically speaking, the reverse chronological and the functional/chronological combination are the strongly preferred choices, since they are what readers expect and they are simplest to write well. A functional resume without a chronology is usually thrown out, because potential employers want to know who an applicant worked for, as well as the applicant's titles and dates of employment (at least for the last ten years).

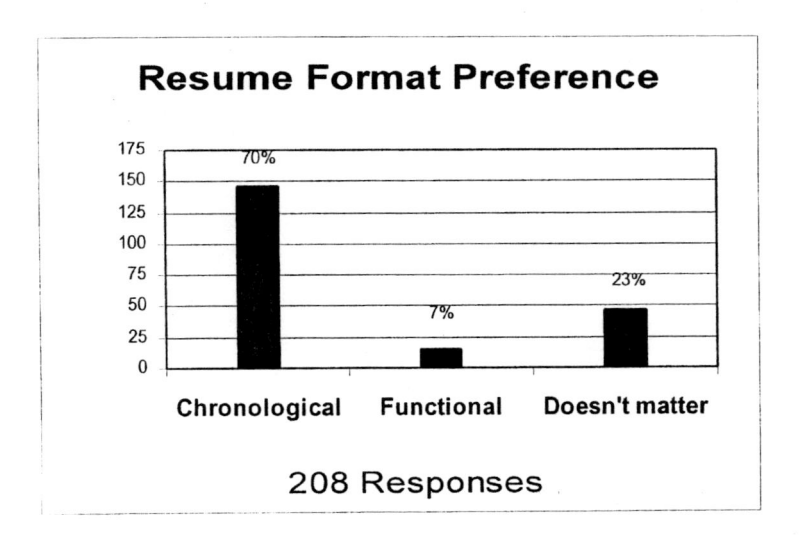

Resume Format Preference

Format	Percentage
Chronological	70%
Functional	7%
Doesn't matter	23%

208 Responses

If you prepare a chronological resume, you will provide a lot of critical information that potential employers want: where you worked, what you did, how long you worked there, and how your career has progressed. However, if you do decide to use a functional resume, make sure that it contains at least some chronological element.

Remember that the readability and overall appearance of a resume are even more important than its format.

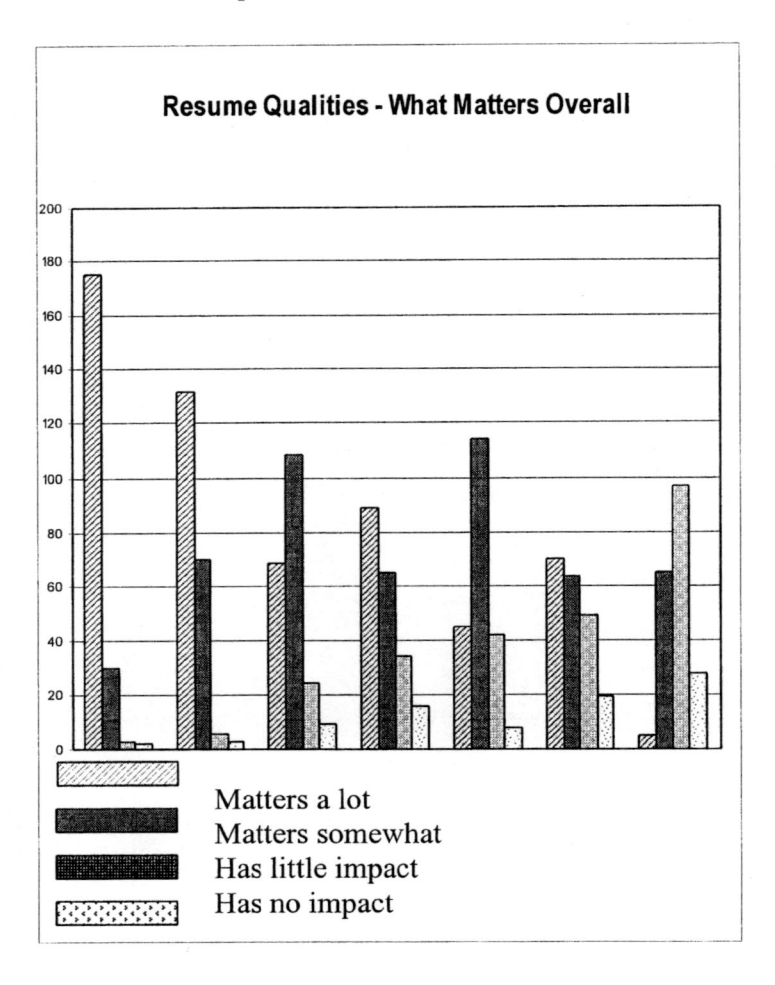

Resume Qualities - What Matters Overall

- Matters a lot
- Matters somewhat
- Has little impact
- Has no impact

Most reviewers scan and eliminate resumes as quickly as possible; in fact, studies suggest that people who review resumes as part of the hiring process spend on average only about 12 to 15 seconds looking at each one. It is critical, therefore, to make your resume as attractive and reader-friendly as possible.

The two sample resumes shown below are fictitious, but demonstrate several key principles and are applicable to many positions. Virtually the only differences are in format.

In the *chronological* version, the applicant is "straight-lining" a job search. The candidate is applying for a job similar to the one held previously, continuing along the same career path.

The *functional* version notes a desire for a career change, and highlights the applicant's transferable skills. This version also lists, but does not lead with, the positions previously held.

Capitalization, bold-face print and eye-catching layout make it easy for readers to scan these resumes in either format. Both styles give quick pictures of what the candidate offers. Also, both make effective use of skill-related nouns and active verbs, and both demonstrate that the candidate has achieved quantifiable results in previous positions.

Functional Format

NAME
Address
Address
Phone
E-mail

PROFILE:

Experienced manager with strong analytical and decision-making skills. Communicate and work well with people. Strong service, team work, customer service and time management skills. Seek position where management, decision making and communication skills can help a firm to be profitable. Fluent in English and Spanish.

> **MANAGEMENT:** Directed a staff of seven. Maintained workflow within the department to be service-oriented. Trained and supervised 22 staff underwriters over a five-year period.
>
> **ANALYSIS AND DECISION MAKING:** Analyzed credit and property risk in $850 million worth of mortgage loan transactions. Approved or rejected claim applications depending on determinations of risk.
>
> **COMMUNICATIONS:** Communicated with branch offices' personnel and accounting staffs to work on problems and achieve agreed decisions.
>
> **MORTGAGE LENDING:** Directed the underwriting of all of the conventional mortgage loan applications which originated in my branch. Worked with branch personnel in the submission of loan packages ranging from $35,000 to $400,000 to ensure quick approval.

PROFESSIONAL EXPERIENCE:

Worked as Manager of Residential Underwriting for Fidelity Bond Corporation (1995-present). Previously worked as a Branch Underwriter for First Virginia Mortgage, Inc., (1989-1995).

EDUCATION:

BA, Political Science, University of Maryland, College Park, MD, 1985.
1989 FNMA Seminar on CONDO/PUD approval process and spot loan programs. Also completed course on General Mortgage Banking through the Philadelphia Mortgage Bankers Association.

PERSONAL:

Enjoy sailing and painting. Experienced using IBM-compatible PCs for word processing, budgeting and other spreadsheet operations (Microsoft Office, Windows 2000, Excel, Adobe). Active volunteer with Literacy Action. Member, Board of Directors, Reading Is Fundamental program.

> Chronological Format

Name
Address
Address
Phone
E-mail

UNDERWRITING MANAGEMENT

PROFILE: Experienced manager with mortgage lending experience as supervisor in all areas of mortgage loan underwriting. Possess strong analytical and decision-making skills. Strengths:

➢ Interpersonal Communication	➢ Adaptable, Flexible
➢ Team Building	➢ Time Management
➢ Customer Relations	➢ Staff Development

➢ Fluent in English and Spanish

PROFESSIONAL EXPERIENCE:

FIDELITY BOND CORPORATION, Arlington, VA, 1995-Present
Manager, Residential Underwriting
Analyzed credit and property risk for $850 million in mortgage loans. Directed an underwriting staff of seven people. Maintained workflow within the department to be service-oriented. Trained and supervised 22 staff underwriters in a five-year period. Analyzed credit and property risk in residential and commercial mortgage loan transactions. Approved or rejected claim applications depending on determinations of risk. Communicated with branch offices' and headquarters' staffs to solve problems and achieve agreed decisions.

FIRST VIRGINIA MORTGAGE, INC., Vienna, VA, 1989-1995
Branch Underwriter
Managed underwriting of all conventional mortgage loan applications which originated in my branch. Worked with branch personnel on the submission of loan packages from $35,000 to $400,000 to ensure quick underwriting approval.

EDUCATION:

BA, Political Science, University of Maryland, College Park, MD, 1989. 1989 FNMA Seminar on CONDO/PUD approval process and spot loan programs. Completed course on General Mortgage Banking through Philadelphia Mortgage Bankers Association.

PERSONAL:

Enjoy sailing and painting. Experienced using PCs for word processing, budgeting and other spreadsheet operations (Microsoft Office, Windows 2000, Excel, Adobe). Active volunteer with Literacy Action. Member, Board of Directors, Reading is Fundamental program.

Creating the Future-Directed Resume

Most resumes are obituaries. They describe what the writer of the resume did for somebody else in the past. But if you are looking for a job *now*, what you need is a future-directed resume that describes what you can do for someone else in the days ahead.

Writing a future-directed resume requires specific answers to the questions, "What do I want to do?" and "What can I do for someone else?" Actually, the second question in its full form would be more like "What can I do for someone else that I am likely to do well and enjoy and get paid to do?"

Most of us need to go through an assessment process to refine answers to those questions. If you can't yet answer them effectively, undertake career assessments to help yourself get focused. Only when you can answer the above questions will you be ready to write your resume. By the time you are able to write it, you should be able to speak it. Remember that a resume is a script of what you want to do, and why you can do it well.

A future-directed, opening statement of objectives sets the tone for the rest of a resume. To be effective, such a statement must be based on a thorough self-assessment.

As a result of assessment, you can focus on things that you do well and want to do. You can eliminate the things that you don't want to do. Listing your strengths can not only emphasize them, but can help an employer relate your skills to the future needs of the organization. Following are some examples of resume openings that include future-directed statements and lists of strengths.

LEGISLATIVE COUNSEL GOVERNMENT RELATIONS
Analysis . . . Policy . . . Federal and State Regulations

Profile: Major trade association and congressional experience. Key legal legislative issues:

Land Use	Congressional Procedures
Emerging Appraiser Regulations	Fair Housing
Federal Budget Process	Secondary Markets
Federal Housing Credit	Banking Legislation
RESPA/Truth in Lending	State and Local Issues

ADMINISTRATIVE ASSISTANT

Profile: Bilingual in English and Spanish; particularly strong in human resources, accounting (benefits, payroll), and administrative functions essential to successful operations of an organization. Strengths:

Flexible	Task and Goal Oriented
Sees Projects to Completion	Accurate with Numbers
Attentive to Detail	Has Sound Judgment
Excellent Attendance Record	Is a Good Listener

COMPUTER TECHNICIAN

Profile: Highly skilled individual with extensive computer experience in maintenance and configuration. Also experienced in electronic repair. Keeps abreast of new hardware and software. Has worked in on-site and field service environments. Strengths:

PC Experience	Troubleshooting
Good Customer Service	Innovative Problem Solving
Helpful to End Users	Thorough and Persistent

In today's job market, flexibility and career development require the ability to present credentials in new areas. Creating a future-directed resume will allow you to raise the bar of expectations and get the reader's attention. Instead of submitting an "obituary" resume solely about your past, send something that shows what you want to do, and can do, for the employer.

Resumes: Stating Objectives and Capitalizing on Gaps in Employment

People often have trouble preparing statements of objectives for their resumes. What do employers expect? Is it necessary to include a statement of objectives in a resume, or can a job seeker omit it and just list education and accomplishments?

Consider your statement of objectives as an index card that summarizes what you do best, what you offer employers, and what you want to do. This statement is convenient for "scanners" of your resume who are searching for a summary of your skills and abilities.

If you are having trouble writing your resume, it may be because you have not focused your search. If you can't prepare a statement succinct enough to fit on an index card, you probably need to do more formal or informal self-assessments to become focused. Fortunately, there are dozens of exercises, instruments and coaches available to help you.

A young man who had taken a year off to travel, and then took another six months to write a book about his experiences, contacted me. In a job interview, the interviewer expressed concern and disappointment that the man had not been "working" for such a long period of time. The young man asked me how he could describe his travel and writing experience in his resume so as to enhance his chances of obtaining employment.

This job seeker was puzzling: he had been adventurous enough to travel for a year, and imaginative and disciplined enough to write a book about his experiences, but was nonetheless unable to take advantage of those qualities in an interview. Here is what I suggested to him.

First, make sure that you yourself view your travel and writing experiences positively. If you don't, it's doubtful others will. There is much to admire in your recent story: you took control of your career, you made a decision to try something radically different, and you did it. Bravo! Too many of us are too faint of heart when it comes to taking personal and career risks.

Second, think about what you saw and heard; whom you met; and what you learned about yourself, others and the world. Then visualize how all of that can increase your value to an employer. After that, you'll need to put those things in written form.

To do so, first write a letter describing what you were doing before your travels, where you went, and what you wrote while traveling. Next, give two or three short examples of what you did on your travels. Then state what you want to do or can do now as a result. Finally, take the best two or three sentences from that letter and put them in your chronological resume to account for the 18 months spent traveling and writing.

A last thought: don't be arrogant or boastful about your accomplishments, but don't worry about people who are bored or threatened by your travels and memoirs. You don't want to work for them anyway!

Another case concerning a gap in employment involved an associate who had been laid off twice within the two previous years on account of downsizing. He wanted to know how to write a resume and cover letter to show that despite periods of unemployment he was not a wanderer, but someone who could be a long-term, dedicated employee.

I urged my associate to address his periods of unemployment directly in a cover letter to accompany his resume. He could write, "Having gone through two downsizings in two years, I am seeking the opportunity to work with a company that is growing." I suggested that he individualize each cover letter, focusing on what the targeted employer needs, wants and is interested in. He could also put a simple sentence at the end of his résumé's entries about those two jobs (e.g., "Entire department was eliminated in a corporate reorganization.")

In handling this delicate issue, it's important not to sound like a whiner or victim. Employers want employees who are sufficiently resilient to cope well with change.

Career Change Process/Special Situations

Singing the Too-Qualified Blues

Many job seekers who are over age 50 complain that it's difficult to get in the door for interviews because they are "too qualified" for certain positions, even though they would seriously consider the positions in question. Some people in that situation have asked me if it's a good idea to "dumb down" their resumes. Further, they wonder if there are any particular things that older job seekers should make sure to include in resumes, cover letters and interviews.

If you think your age will work against you in the job market, you are probably right. But don't sabotage your job search with negative thoughts! Take heart: "baby boomers" and other oldsters are staying in the workforce. Studies show that as of 2006, close to 40% of American workers are 45 years old or older. [vii]

I have always considered "too qualified" a euphemistic way of saying, "I don't want to hire you and it's easier to compliment your qualifications and scoot you out the door than tell you the real reason I don't want to hire you." But why do some employers shy away from hiring older people? It's because there are a number of real or imagined liabilities associated with age: decreased physical and mental abilities, obsolete skills and knowledge, increased illnesses and absences, higher salary and health-care costs, and alleged stubbornness and inability to work with younger people.

The key is to counter these preconceptions. Are you staying fit physically and mentally? Are you staying current in skills and information? Are you expanding your horizons of interest, experience and knowledge? Are you able to convey those realities in interviews and networking conversations?

Older people are more active and living longer than any previous generation could have imagined. Age is an advantage in terms of work ethic, general knowledge, experience, wisdom, strength of convictions, ability to mentor young staff members, and business skills applicable to business needs.

With regard to "dumbing down" a resume: if this means understating your capabilities and accomplishments, and making yourself appear less valuable than you really are, then, "NO!" On the other hand, it's good to focus your resume on a particular area you want to emphasize, while downplaying skills and abilities that you are less interested in using. In crafting your resume, make sure that it is future-directed to show where you want to go, what you can do and what you want to do.

Finally, remember that salary questions are essentially questions about money, not age. If you have stayed current in skills, knowledge and ability, you should be looking for jobs that pay appropriately.

Establishing Credibility Without a College Degree

How important is a college degree in the world of business management? I once was asked this question by a man who had successfully managed offices and run businesses. Seeking to advance his career, he applied for a job he really wanted, went through five interviews, but was rejected in the end because, he said, he did not have a college degree.

It seemed to me that he had failed to appreciate the fact that employers have limited time to sort through resumes and meet with applicants. In business, time is money. Degrees are a form of shorthand, telling an interviewer in a matter of seconds what an applicant's educational credentials are.

Credentials establish standards. A degree or diploma, for instance, can indicate qualifications. It quickly informs the interviewer that an applicant has an education in a specific field, has set goals and met them, is able to research and analyze information, and can communicate reasonably well.

In his case, the interviewer had a dilemma. The applicant apparently had the interpersonal and management skills that the firm required, and he had a good track record, but he was unable to convince the company that his personality, experience and accomplishments made him the best applicant for the job even without a college degree.

I suggested that for the next time, he make a list of all of his formal and informal education and training. More would be better here, particularly if he could stress educational experiences that relate to the type of position for which he was applying. If the job is to manage an office, he should emphasize whatever training and education he has had in administration, budgeting, scheduling, organization, negotiating, supervising and computer use. If the work involves broader management responsibilities, he should stress recruiting, training, supervising, marketing, setting goals and achieving results.

He should mention courses, workshops and self-study in his resume or cover letter. If he has had any undergraduate work he should describe it as "undergraduate studies" or "studied English and business at . . ." Or he might simply list the school(s) and subjects studied without indicating a degree.

His approach to any interview should be designed to help the prospective employer to conclude that although he does not have an undergraduate degree, *he is a desirable candidate because he has considerable training and education in the areas the position requires.*

Finally, anyone who needs professional assistance should check with the American College Advisory Service (which works with another organization known as ED Vising). It may be reached on the Internet at:

http://www.brwm.org/americancollegeadvisoryservice.

This organization can help you recall and record your experience. It can also help you to find an appropriate institution that will accept experience as part of degree requirements, and will work with you to create a study program which will allow you to complete your degree without unnecessary expenditure of money and time.

Transitioning Out of Human Resources: Many Options

Not long ago, I was contacted by a human resources expert, who stated that after ten years in the HR field, she had decided to move into something not HR-related. She asked what her options might be, what steps she should take, and what I thought of the likelihood of her success in transitioning to a new kind of work.

It appeared to me that her background in human resources had helped her develop in-depth skills, knowledge and competencies that could easily be applied in other careers. Over the years, I have had the satisfaction of helping many human resources professionals to move successfully into new careers.

If you are thinking about moving out of the field of human resources to a new career or industry, first figure out where you want to live and work. Assess what you do well, what you enjoy, and how you can translate that into other positions. While this is simple to say, it may be rather complex and time-consuming to accomplish. It will be a good investment in time and effort for you to take a few weeks to figure out what you want to do in the next phase of your career.

While there are undoubtedly many industries, and many types of careers, in which you could find satisfying and remunerative work, you might want to focus initially on positions that draw upon the skills you have developed in the field of human resources. In all probability, those include:

- Communicating effectively with others,
- Leading, managing and motivating others,
- Presenting ideas and convincing others of their value and usefulness,
- Listening effectively, and
- Drafting letters and memoranda.

Those skills are of course very useful in many types of work, including the following:

- Business development,
- Organizational development,
- Project management,
- Writing, editing and publishing,
- Operations and administrative management,
- Budgeting and planning,
- Ensuring and documenting compliance with legal requirements, including federal, state and local laws and regulations,
- Career counseling and coaching,
- Search, recruitment and placement,
- Non-profit organization management,
- Training and meeting facilitation, and
- Human resources consulting.

Once you have determined your preferred geographic location, and have inventoried your skills, you can establish goals, prepare a resume, and begin your search.

If you are considering a career change that involves moving from one function to another, one industry to another, or a combination of both, keep in mind that it is usually easier to change one of those at a time, rather than both together. In other words, consider a position in your functional specialty but in a different industry, or stay in the industry you're now in, and move to a new function within it.

A final tip: if you have any inclinations toward sales, business development or revenue generation, consider acting on those inclinations. Busy executives are more likely to want to talk with a prospective employee who has the potential to generate revenue, than with one who is likely just to consume it.

Transitioning from the Federal Government to the Private Sector

Many people who have worked in the Federal Government have little difficulty adapting their skills to the non-governmental world. For example, an assistant press secretary on Capitol Hill might find similar positions in public relations, media relations or external affairs.

If, for instance, in your current (or a past) government job you wrote press releases, researched media outlets and answered press inquiries, you would do well to search for positions that require writing, editing, research, customer service or media relations. The idea is to identify the skills you used in government, and then match those skills with specific jobs in the private sector. Career assessments can help you to identify your skills (and interests) and can help you turn them into a marketable resume.

Most human resources managers have large workloads. The first things they look for when reviewing a stack of resumes are *dis*qualifiers — reasons to eliminate candidates. Make sure you are not selected out and that you pass that initial screening.

To do that, focus on your primary self-marketing vehicle — your resume. Make sure that it is well written, error-free and future-directed. Your resume provides its readers with their first impressions of you, and it is thus a key factor in getting you in the door.

Make sure that your resume conveys a clear and concise message, showing organizations what you can do for them. Write a future-directed resume that describes your skills and abilities, but do so in language and terminology that a non-governmental executive can understand. After you have described your past work experience in terms of your current abilities, compose your resume with reference to those talents. Highlight specific examples from the position(s) you had in government. By keeping your resume future-directed, you will show decision makers in private organizations how you could help them. In other words, a good future-directed resume will give prospective employers reasons they should hire you.

The following is an example of a future-directed resume statement for an executive.

INTERNATIONAL DEVELOPMENT EXECUTIVE

Profile: Development professional with proven record of running overseas and domestic development programs. Possesses experience in international and domestic locations. Excels at training and motivating staff. A skilled negotiator able to cut through obstacles and reach winning compromises. Especially skilled at developing and implementing programs, justifying and managing financial plans, and facilities improvement and site planning. Other skills include problem solving and evaluation. Fluent in Spanish, with some knowledge of German, Russian and French.

The next future-directed statement applies to members of support staff.

EXECUTIVE SECRETARY

Profile: Experienced international executive secretary with solid skills in communication, public relations, management and research. Strong in administrative functions essential to successful operation of an organization. Fluent in Spanish, French and Italian.

Such future-directed statements can help you apply the skills you developed in the federal government to the private sector. The *content* of your resume is not the only thing to consider, however; the overall *appearance* is also critical to the success of your resume.

In a survey conducted by Morris Associates, Inc., human resources managers, hiring managers and recruiters indicated that with regard to resumes, readability and overall appearance matter most.

Although the readability and appearance of resumes were found to be most significant, typos, font-size and quality of paper were also considered important. One respondent wrote, "Your resume is the first impression, so make sure it is well organized, neat, easy to read, and has no typos."

Remember that your resume should use action verbs (e.g. created, organized, coordinated, drafted, led) to explain your role in the success of a project. State your skills clearly, making sure to show quantitative results when appropriate; show how your past experience demonstrates those skills; and tie your skills to the needs and goals of your prospective employer. Use phrases and examples like:

➢ *cut* costs _____ percent,
➢ *managed* staff of _____,
➢ *developed* $ _____ budget,
➢ *wrote* _____ -page report,
➢ *coordinated* _____ -person team, and
➢ *managed* office move of _____ -person staff to new _____ -square foot facility.

Consider the relative dynamism of the following two statements:

> Through an innovative major hiring effort, there was a significant improvement in the overall productivity of my department in which I was considered a major contributor.
>
> Recruited, interviewed, hired staff of 15 quality control technicians. Increased assembly output 17% in six months while reducing error rate by 4%.

If you use quantitative information as in the second example, you will drive your past accomplishments home and show what you have to offer your future employer. Using that sort of specificity, you can make great first impressions and get interviews.

Should I Stay or Should I Go?

Recently I was contacted by a man who had decided to pursue a Master's Degree in his field, thinking that an advanced degree would make him more appreciated and valued within the association where he was working. He sensed that his boss was threatened by the development of his educational and professional skills and that he was being assigned less interesting work than before.

He had entered his organization ten years earlier as an administrative assistant and had received a few promotions. He felt, however, that he was still regarded as administrative staff, even though he had performed management-level work for some years. He was upset that he was not being compensated appropriately for his management work.

He reported that he had tried approaching his boss several times to discuss how he might improve his standing in the organization, but to no avail. Feeling demoralized, he wondered if he should try to make a lateral move.

In discussing this situation with him, I told him that several times in my own career, I had taken jobs that failed to mesh my values and abilities with the organizations' missions and needs. Early on in these situations, I tried expressing my concerns to key decision makers. When things still weren't working out, I agonized, lost sleep and spent weekends dreading the weeks ahead.

From this, I learned to trust my instincts. I took stock of my professional career, analyzed my options, updated my resume and started job searches. One time, my job situation became so unsatisfactory that I quit even before I was able to begin a job search. I don't usually recommend that, but sometimes tough decisions have to be made.

I have never regretted any decision to leave a job. In some cases it took a while to find my next position, but there always *was* a next position, and it was usually better suited to my skills and interests than the previous one.

Of course, making a career change these days entails risks, since stability and security in the job market aren't to be assumed anymore.

So, should you go or should you stay? My advice is, don't stay in a job you hate. If you cannot move up or over, move on.

Why December May Be the Best Month for a Job Search

Every year as winter approaches, I field calls from professionals who are ready to plan their next career moves. A common question is whether it is reasonable to launch an actual job search between Thanksgiving and the winter holidays. As one professional put it, "Should I just bag my efforts until January, or is there another approach I should consider?"

My advice is that, contrary to fairly widespread belief, December may actually be the best month to conduct a job search. There are at least five reasons for this.

Less Competition: Since so many people believe December is a bad month to look for a job, they don't actively search during that month. Hence, there is less competition from other job seekers, and potential employers have more time to consider those who do apply for positions.

More Access: "Everybody" does not go away for the December holidays. On the contrary, many managers are both catching up on unfinished business and are getting ready for the new year. Many human resources directors are working on staffing plans for the coming year, and are more attentive to personnel matters than they usually are. Thus the last month of the year can be the best month of all to get access to key people.

The Giving Season: As people get in the spirit of the year-end holidays, they tend to be more disposed toward helping others. There may not be a huge swing in this direction, but even a little increased openness by hiring managers works in favor of applicants.

January Hires: January is often one of the biggest months of the year for hiring. However, individuals who are hired in January usually are not the people who waited until then to start their job searches. Those hired in January are often people who were actively pursuing leads in December. (I've worked with job applicants who had critical interviews on Christmas Eve or during the last week of the year.)

The January Rush: A lot of people make New Year's resolutions to change jobs. In January, therefore, the market becomes more saturated with job seekers. If you put off your search until after the December holidays, you're likely to have to compete with a bigger (and possibly more determined) crowd in January. You also risk losing psychological job-search momentum around Thanksgiving, and you may not get into high gear until mid-or-late January. That means, obviously, that a job seeker can actually lose two months, not just one, by suspending activity in December.

Company Layoffs: Surviving and Thriving

Change is an inevitable aspect of life, including working life. We can be successful in dealing with change by being attentive to signs that change is coming, by preparing for it, by keeping a positive mental attitude in the face of uncertainty, and by being alert to new opportunities.

Here are some major signs that layoffs may be coming:

- New directors and/or executive staff are moving in.
- There are more closed-door meetings than previously.
- The number of staff meetings is increasing.
- There are mounting indications of poor performance or low work output.
- Rumors of impending changes have begun to circulate.
- Other organizations in the same field are downsizing.
- Leaders in the same field are "repositioning" for new market efforts.

If you think that major changes are in store for your organization, and if you decide to try to remain there, these tips may help you:

- Be familiar with your organization's culture.
- Know the organization's core competencies.
- Evaluate how you measure up in terms of those core competencies.
- Make sure the new executive team knows who you are, as well as what you've done and *can do* for the organization.
- If your office is reducing the number of staff members, find out all you can about the new leaders and how they do business. Observe and be prepared to fit into the new culture which they will bring.
- Make yourself valuable. Be prepared to demonstrate to the new managers that you can contribute to smooth-running operations, and that you can work well and productively with others.

- Get your work done in a timely, accurate fashion.
- Stay abreast of developments in your field, and keep your technical skills current.
- Broaden the scope and range of what you do. Do not isolate yourself or confine your work to a narrow job description.
- Be a team player, not a lone wolf. Seek opportunities to work as part of interdepartmental teams or on committees.

But suppose it's time to leave? It's good to have a plan of action in the event that your organization decides to let you go, or if you decide that it's time for you to move on. These suggestions may help you in such a career change:

- Be positive when speaking with co-workers. Pay attention to rumors but don't spread them.
- Know your career goals and be prepared to articulate them succinctly.
- Update your resume, making sure that it is focused on the future.
- Make a list of key contacts and stay in touch with them.
- Send "thank-you" and "congratulations" notes to people you know when appropriate.

You may run into portrayals of American workers as victims: feeble, dependent, unresourceful, unimaginative and unable to cope with changes or setbacks. Some analysts say that disappointments along our career paths often lead to denial, anger, panic, depression, and drug and alcohol abuse.

But I have seen a happier side of this. As a career transition counselor for more than 25 years, I have worked with thousands of individuals. Even though many had a difficult time initially accepting the reality of having been laid off, and although most of them didn't enjoy the process of searching for new work (how many people do?), many moved quickly to new and satisfying employment. In fact, a significant percentage of those people came to view their situations as career advancement opportunities, while some of them changed careers altogether with no loss of job satisfaction.

The truth is that many American workers are fully able to recognize and accept career changes. They make commitments to move on with their lives, and they do so successfully.

So my final suggestion is, KEEP A POSITIVE ATTITUDE!

Networking, Interviewing and Negotiating

Networking and Interviewing

Some books on job searching, and many career consultants, present an overly complicated picture of the job search process. Some stress using the phone, networking, and getting through or around the personnel department. Others stress asking, listening, gathering information and doing research. There is also the marketing approach: analysis of background, positioning and targeting, researching, creating communications materials, strategizing, practicing interviews, campaign planning and implementation.

Winning a new job can be tough work. But does it also have to be complicated? Do most people have to go through all of the steps mentioned above when they change jobs? The answer is no.

Job hunting becomes complicated when a person is unemployed or working in a job that is not stimulating. Unemployment diminishes a person's marketability: the probability that people will hire you drops if you're not in a job while looking for another one.

Unemployment breeds insecurity. Underemployment — being unsatisfied and not challenged in a job — leads to insecurity as well. Insecure people don't usually win job offers, especially at the management level. Sometimes a key to a successful career is to avoid underemployment.

Networking

If you do wind up unemployed, avoid rejection. You can do that by seeking information, rather than directly looking for a job.

How People Find Jobs[iii]

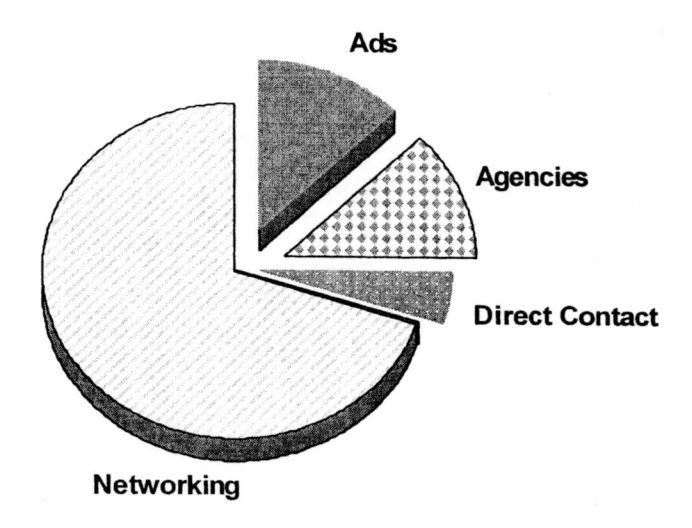

- Ads
- Agencies
- Direct Contact
- Networking

Speak to someone in the industry, firm or position that you are seeking. Ask for comments on your resume. Get as much information as you can about the industry, the company, and the people with whom you'll be meeting.

Remember, you are not asking for a job. If there are no job openings, most likely the person with whom you are meeting will tell you so. If there are job openings and the person is not informing you of them, the odds are there is bad chemistry between the two of you. An excellent way to improve chemistry in a meeting or interview is to ask intelligent questions and be a good listener. *Try to put the focus on the employer's future.*

Some questions you could ask:

- I understand your firm's major competitors are x, y and z. How/why is your firm better than these?
- Your annual report mentioned that acquisitions will be a major part of your growth strategy this year; how is that strategy progressing?
- Describe the company's basic management philosophy.
- What is the major issue facing the company?
- What are the challenges facing your company?
- Is the company meeting its objectives?
- The *Wall Street Journal* mentioned that your firm might be acquired by x company. Do you think that will happen? If it did, what impact would it have on the position we are discussing?
- What does it take to be successful in this organization?
- Does my resume speak to the organization's needs?
- How could my skills best fit into your firm's operations?
- Which are the growth firms in your industry?
- Why do you work here? How did you get your job?
- In what ways has this organization been most successful in terms of products and services over the years?
- How would you describe the culture here?
- Where do you see the company (or position) going in the next few years?
- What significant changes do you foresee in the near future?
- Does the company sponsor personal or professional courses, seminars or meetings?
- In what areas do you see the biggest payoff occurring if some problems were solved?

- What are the basic values that make up the company's culture?
- Is the company growing? If so, where is growth coming from?
- What are the most critical factors for success in your business?
- How long have you been with the firm/organization?
- What obstacles do you see that may prevent you from meeting your objectives?
- What do you think has to happen to bring this company/department to the next level?
- How do you see this being accomplished?
- What are your top two goals for the future?
- What are your plans for this department?
- What do you like here? What do you dislike?
- If you could be freed up here to do anything you wanted to do, what would you do?
- What would you need to be freed up from to do that?
- Can you tell me how you have progressed in your career within this organization?
- How did your affiliation with the company begin?
- How would you describe your own management style?
- How do you like the company?
- Where do you see yourself going in the next two years?
- Would you introduce me to the person who does the hiring?

In this series, only the last question might produce rejection.

Future-Directed Resumes

Another essential component of the job search is having a future-directed resume. Most resumes tell what you have already done. What you need to do now is write a resume that says what you can do for someone else. A good resume is future-directed.

Writing a future-directed resume requires clear answers to the questions, "What do I want to do?" and "What can I do for someone else?" (Actually, the complete second question is, "What can I do for someone else that I am likely to do well, enjoy and get paid well for doing?")

When you can answer the above questions, you are ready to write your resume. By the time you are able to write it, you should be able to speak it. A resume is a script of what you want to do and why you can do it well. Once it is written, the best thing to do with it is to commit it to conversation and go get a job. The resume, once written, has served its most useful purpose, that of focusing you on where you are going and what skills, accomplishments, experiences and education you bring with you to accomplish new successes.

If you don't go into your search with a knowledgeable and positive view of yourself, you will have a hard time winning satisfying offers.

Interviewing

Hiring decisions are instinctual, based heavily on impressions. Impressions are made in minutes, sometimes seconds, at the beginning of interviews.

If you are nervous, you might say so. Interviewers are often nervous too. Just as most of us have not been trained to be interviewed, most managers have not been trained to interview.

Always enter an interview with the intention of winning an offer. Don't judge a firm too hastily. If the chemistry seems bad between you and the other person, it may be temporary. The other person may be having a bad day. If the person is serious about considering you, he or she may challenge you to see how you perform under stress. Tension in an interview can be a good sign; it can mean you are being considered.

If you want the job, say so. And send an upbeat note of thanks after every meeting.

Offers are not jobs. There are three steps to winning a new job: get in for the interview; go for an offer; and when you get an offer, negotiate it into the job.

Remember: go for an offer, not a job. You can negotiate an offer into a better deal for yourself if you know how to negotiate for authority, responsibility, resources and remuneration. Potential employers usually have flexibility in at least one or two of these areas.

Negotiating is good interviewing practice. You can turn down any offers you don't want, but you can't turn down any offers you don't get. Your goal should be to get an offer.

The image you project and the chemistry between you and the interviewer are 70% of winning the job offer. Skills and ability account for 30% in winning an offer. Skills are important. If you don't have appropriate skills, experience, or other qualifiers in your background, you probably won't be considered. However, skills and abilities are not enough.

To the above, add 10% for perseverance and 10% for luck, with luck defined as preparation and opportunity. (There's a lot of truth in the adage, "The harder you work, the luckier you get.") That adds up to 120%, which is the amount of effort you have to put into winning a good job.

Where To Network

- Business/professional contacts.
- Industry contacts.
- Friends/family/neighbors.
- Academic/social contacts.
- People who depend on you for income.
- Church/volunteer groups.
- People in your card file/address book.
- Former employers/co-workers.
- Everywhere: your resume is your script.

Finding a Job by Associating with Associations

> "Americans are an enterprising people. Whenever two or more of them have a common purpose, they form a society."
>
> *Alexis De Tocqueville*[ix]

Yes, like-minded Americans love to form associations wherein people who have common interests can discuss them, and can work together to advance shared goals. As is well known, associations represent their members' interests to state and federal government agencies, media outlets and the general public. But associations have an oft-overlooked additional benefit: they constitute perhaps the single greatest avenue for contact with, and information about, fields of interest to career seekers.

Through contacts with associations, people looking for new jobs can identify important leaders with interests similar to their own. A job search which includes networking through associations stands a very good chance of success. And there are several easy-to-use tools at hand to help anyone who wants to become acquainted with associations in any field.

Of all the aids available to job seekers and career changers, one of the best is the *Encyclopedia of Associations*.[x] Even more valuable than the encyclopedia itself is the wealth of resources and information to which it can lead.

Another great resource for identifying associations is the *National Trade and Professional Associations of the United States Directory* (NTPA).[xi] With this tool, our large and diverse population has easy access to the leaders, influencers, employers and decision makers in any field. Whether you're interested in aardvark farming or zymurgy or something in between, the NTPA directory is bound to be a helpful resource for making contacts.

A client recently told us that she was interested in transitioning from marketing to public relations, but was unsure where to look. Together we looked at the *Encyclopedia of Associations* and found there were a total of 96 listings relevant to people in her situation. The entries ranged from the Public Relations Society of America to a group called Women Executives in Public Relations.

Interested in horses? The NTPA directory lists a total of 316 horse-related associations ranging from the American Academy of Equestrian Art to the World Arabian Horse Organization. Interested in landscaping? There are 43 landscaping-related associations mentioned in the directory.

Using the indexes of the associations described in the *Encyclopedia of Associations* or the NTPA directory, you can identify which ones match your interests. The two books contain synopses describing each listed association, with information on when the association was founded, its leadership, the number of its members, its annual budget, and points of contact for those who want to learn more about the organization. In addition, an association's synopsis lists the association's professional interest sections, publications, and conferences.

Once you have identified an association of possible interest to you, find out if the group has a local chapter, call the president or membership chair, and attend a meeting. Introduce yourself at the meeting, and network. You or anyone using this approach can become well versed in any industry within a few weeks.

The client who wanted to move from marketing to public relations did her homework. From the list of public relations associations we identified, she selected several to contact. Within weeks she had developed a network of people who provided her with useful information and contacts. Within two months, she had several good offers.

So, to add power to your job search, look up your field of interest in one of the directories mentioned above, and then call or e-mail some associations in that field. Better yet, join one or more of those associations, and you'll soon be well connected!

Dances with Interviews

Some prospective employers use phone interviews as their first points of contact with job applicants, and consider that a phone interview is a first screening. Many job seekers wonder how to handle phone interviews. How much information should an applicant volunteer? What should an applicant say to get in the door for a face-to-face interview?

It is also fairly common for prospective employers, especially human resources people in non-profit organizations, to use panels to interview prospective employees. Some applicants are uncertain as to how to prepare for such an interview, and how to behave during the process.

With any type of interview, a positive attitude and careful preparation are most important.

To prepare, first do your research. What do you know about the employer? The interviewers? The employer's needs? The position? The decision-making process necessary to make the hire? Which of your skills, abilities, experiences and personal traits are most likely to be sought by the employer? What are the employer's "hot buttons"? The more you know about the answers to these questions, the better prepared you will be to do well in your interviews.

Before an interview, prepare a strong opening statement that links your experience and abilities with the prospective employer's needs. Be prepared to state examples of your work that demonstrate that you have skills and competencies that the interviewer's firm needs. Have good questions to ask.

Phone Interviews

The ability to deal well with people on the phone is a requirement of almost every job at every level. A telephone interview is a good chance for you to demonstrate your phone communications skills.

Face-to-face communication consists of three elements: words, tone of voice and body language. But when you are communicating by telephone, there is no observable body language. So the words you use and your tone of voice become much more important, as does your ability to listen and respond.

The words you use on the telephone should be positive. Use words like challenge, solution, success, opportunity, responsible and excellent. Avoid words like can't, won't, don't, haven't, unsuccessful, failure, problem, bad, unemployed and fired.

Stand while doing a phone interview. Smile into the phone. The tone of your voice should be clear and enthusiastic. Don't sound disinterested, mumble words or be monotonous in your tone. Don't chew gum, smoke or eat during a phone interview.

Group Interviews

Group interviews are commonly used by associations, as well as academic and other non-profit organizations that screen job applicants through the use of boards of directors, or peer-selection committees. Group interviews are usually arranged for senior executives and professionals. At those high levels, most position requirements include presentation skills, and a group interview is a valuable chance to demonstrate those skills.

Group interviewers tend to ask tough questions (e.g. "You don't have experience in our fields; why should we select you over candidates who do?", "You've had a lot of jobs, wouldn't you say?" and "Why haven't you secured a new position yet?"). Be prepared to address such questions.

When responding to a question, speak directly to the person who asked it. Maintain eye contact with the person who asked the question, but don't ignore the others. If members of an interview panel have differences, avoid taking sides. Get business cards of panelists so you can send follow-up letters. At the end of the interview, express interest in the position for which you have interviewed if you want it, and confirm the next steps in the process.

Note to interviewers: If you are conducting a group interview, pay attention to things you can do to make interviewees more comfortable. That will demonstrate your organization's consideration for its employees. In particular, make sure that the interviewee has a comfortable chair with a table in front of it. Bottled water should be within easy reach.

The Etiquette of References

The handling of references can involve sensitive issues of propriety. Some of those issues were raised in a letter I recently received from a young man who was angry at himself and perplexed as to his next move, because of the way he had handled a request from a potential employer for references. Here's what he wrote:

> I've made a big mistake. I lost my last association job about a year ago and have been temping since then. I just had a good shot at another position that I really wanted with a non-profit. After the first interview, which went well in my opinion, I was asked for references, including the name of the person I worked for in my last job.
>
> My last boss and I didn't see eye-to-eye and I knew I wouldn't get a good reference from him, so instead of giving his name to my interviewer I said that I had worked under someone else in my former organization. (In fact, that other person and I had worked well together, although in different departments, on a couple of projects.)
>
> I was one of two finalists for the job with the non-profit, but I wasn't selected. I don't know whether my references were really checked, but I'm bummed. Granted, I didn't handle the situation properly, but I'm sure I'm not the only one who's left a job without a good reference from an immediate supervisor. Would it have been alright for me to have given the name of my supervisor's boss, who saw my performance differently? If so, how much detail do I owe my prospective employer?

This letter brings to mind some guidelines for references:

1. Be pro-active with regard to references before you need them. Select four or five people who know you and your work, and who you believe will give good references. Send or give them copies of your resume, then visit or call them. Make sure they know that you are now looking for a position in specified areas, and that you hope they will be able to give you positive references related to those areas. Get a sense of whether the people you approach for references are enthusiastic about the idea, or if they are reserved and cautious. Select as references the most promising three or four of the people on your list.

2. Have a typed list of the references which you can give out if you are asked. Include names, titles, postal and e-mail addresses, and telephone and FAX numbers. You might add one sentence for each reference describing how the person knows of your work, but that is not necessary. The list should be neatly typed on the same stationery-quality letterhead you use for your resume.

3. Don't put a list of references in or with your resume. Absent some important reason, don't give out your list of references. If you automatically give your references out or put them on your resume, you have no control over who calls them, for what, or when. However, if you only give the names of your references when they are asked for, you can (and should) call each person whose name you gave. Let your references know to whom you have given their names, what the desired position is, and what you think are the keys to winning that position.

4. After you have given the names of any references to a prospective employer, ask the people whom you have listed as references to let you know if the prospective employer contacts them. Alternatively, volunteer to follow up in about a week to see if they have been called. That way you will get feedback on the progress of your candidacy.

Now, back to the "mistake" made by the distraught correspondent mentioned above. I suggested that he call and even try to visit his ex-boss to mend fences, and to see what kind of reference he or she might still be willing to give. Very often, once people are apart and don't have to work together, it is easier to "let bygones be bygones," in favor of positive memories and favorable words about each other. I urged the young job seeker not to give up, but rather to learn from his mistake and move forward.

Of course, it's understandable that the young man who wrote to me was very disappointed that he didn't land the job he wanted, but maybe it just wasn't meant to be. However, I pointed out to him that no harm could come from his writing a positive letter to the target firm, and I urged him to do so. I proposed that he tell his contact in the firm that while he was sorry that he was not selected, he thought that the firm was a fine one, and he would like the opportunity to work there if any other possibilities were to open in the future. I have had several clients who have won offers (and many others who have won respect) by sending such letters.

The ABC's of Executive Compensation

Often job seekers will expend great amounts of time and energy trying to get a job, but when they are actually offered a position, they have little or no idea of what pay and benefits are appropriate, nor how to negotiate appropriate compensation. Here are some key points to negotiating compensation packages successfully.

1. *Know your worth in the marketplace.* What does your field pay? Below are some helpful sources:

>   www.salarysurvey.com
>   www.collegegrad.com/salaries
>   www.salaryexpert.com
>   www.monster.com – salary wizard
>   www.payscale.com

2. *Conduct company-specific research.* Finding wide pay ranges for the sort of responsibilities a new position is likely to have is easy. It is also important to understand the ranges used by the companies you've targeted. Try to learn as much as you can about the salary ranges and compensation packages in effect at each firm to which you apply.

- If you're working with a recruiter, he/she might be a source of information.
- If you know someone inside a target firm, see if that person may be able to help.
- If you're invited back for a second interview, ask prior to that interview for any available literature on the company's benefits and compensation plans. Review that material carefully before the second meeting.
- You'll want to have a solid understanding of the firm's compensation packages for employees at your level, the firm's 401K plans, vesting time frames, the health care program, and other perks like life insurance and vacations.

- Be prepared to ask how the firm's compensation package is structured for a person at your level. You'll want to know about base, bonuses, stock plans, profit sharing, commissions, hiring bonuses, relocation benefits, etc. Other perks such as parking, transportation, and tuition reimbursement (sometimes available for college-bound children), may represent valuable benefits in addition to your salary. There may also be special packages for "selected executives." If so, find out if you would be one of those executives.

   3. *Prepare for salary negotiations.* If you're working with a recruiter, decide if he/she will handle the negotiations, or if you will. Questions and answers about salary negotiation fall into two categories, those related to the past and those pointing to the future.

   Past: What is your salary history? What were your base and your total compensation?

   Future: What salary are you looking for? What do you want?

   You can answer a "future" question with a "past" answer, or a "past" question with a "future" answer. For example:

   Future Question – Past Answer:
   Q. What salary are you looking for?

   A. In my last position, I made X compensation. Of course, I want to get at least that and I'm actually looking to improve that. What's the range for this position?

   Past Question – Future Answer:
   Q. What is your salary history?

A. Given my current obligations, I'm looking for an annual compensation package around X.

If you get an offer that you consider to be low, go to the "Three Loves and a But" tactic. The three loves are: the company, the people and the job.

You prove your interest by saying: "I really *love* the company (for these reasons), the people I've met (for these reasons) and the job (because of what I can contribute — be specific), *but* I do have some salary concerns." Then be silent and let them talk; their response may indicate how interested they are.

If the discussion seems to be stalled, ask: "How can we work this out?" or "You're talking about x compensation. I'm looking more at X compensation. How can we reach an agreement?"

Some things that may be negotiable:

- Vacation (at least one extra week)
- Relocation bonus or hiring bonus, and
- Other potentially valuable non-salary perks.

Finally, below are several excellent books on executive compensation.

Balsam, Steven. *An Introduction to Executive Compensation*. San Francisco: Academic Press, 2002.

Chapman, Jack. *Negotiating Your Salary: How to Make $1000 a Minute*. Berkeley: Ten Speed Press, 1996.

Davis, Michael L. and Jerry T. Edge. *Executive Compensation: The Professional's Guide to Current Issues and Practices*. San Diego: Windsor Professional Information, 2004.

Ellig, Bruce R. *The Complete Guide to Executive Compensation.* New York: McGraw-Hill, 2002.

Rapport, Alfred. *Harvard Business Review on Compensation.* Boston: HBS Press, 2001.

Lucht, John. *Rites of Passage at $100,000 to $1 Million+: Your Insider's Lifetime Guide to Executive Job-Changing and Faster Career Progress in the 21st Century.* New York: Viceroy Press, 1988.

Interviews and Offers

A few years ago, I was contacted by a job seeker who had searched unsuccessfully for several months, and then was suddenly invited to two interviews and several promising network meetings with top executives in New York City. The man in question said that he didn't know what his interviewers' firms wanted or needed. The correspondent asked me, "What should I focus on? How should I sell myself?"

I suggested that he let go of the idea that his purpose in the meetings was "to sell himself" (a distasteful phrase). His objectives should be to listen, to find out what his interviewers' needs were, and then to visualize how he might match his skills and experiences with those needs. By asking questions and listening, he would be able to find out what his interviewers wanted, what they needed, and why they had decided to meet with him.

Could you imagine going to an automobile showroom and having a salesman immediately start showing you cars without asking you questions? You would expect him to find out whether you are just looking or planning to buy; what kind of vehicle you drive now; what other vehicles you're looking at; how you will use the vehicle; the style, safety and extra features that are important to you; and so on. The same is true in a job interview or a networking meeting. You don't go in trying to "sell" yourself before you find out what your potential employer wants. After you determine that, make a judgment as to whether your skills and desires make for a good match; if so, describe that match to the interviewers.

Another dilemma arises when a job seeker unexpectedly receives two or more offers at or near the same time. Choosing between or among job offers can be the most stressful part of a job search. If you are looking to change jobs and need to make such a choice, a good way to start the decision process would be to recall your thoughts and feelings at the time you decided to seek a change. Ask:

- Why did you want to change?
- What did you want to change?
- What working and lifestyle conditions have you been seeking?
- What are your career goals?
- What areas do you need or want to learn or develop in order to further those career goals?

You need to assess not only your skills, knowledge and experience but also what you do and don't want in your next job. Make a list of key factors, values, working conditions and lifestyle considerations that are most important to you. Prioritize the list, and then compare the elements of each offer with the entries on your list.

Because selecting among offers needs to be a "head *and* heart" decision, it will be useful for you to talk to other people about your comparisons of the positions, and about your feelings concerning them. Writing your list gives you the rational framework for your decision, while talking about your feelings will help you see the emotional context for it.

SECTION II

Guidance for Employees

*Ultimately, you are
responsible for your own career.*

-Article page 88

In the Workplace

Communicating with Difficult Bosses or Supervisors

One of the most frequently asked career-related questions revolves around what to do about "bad" bosses. Some of the participants in an on-line discussion hosted by *The Washington Post* asked me questions on that topic. Below is some of what I was asked to comment on.

From one unhappy employee: "What do you do if you have a difficult boss? I know that there's more I could do at this job, but my boss is so hard to work with that she just kills my motivation. I get so sick of her abuse; she snaps at me and then is nice to me. I just end up putting my head down and praying for the day to be over . . . I do the assignments she gives me, but I don't make a move to venture out and tell her about good ideas that I have. She shoots down everything I say, and even when she asks for my opinion, things always are done completely her way anyway. I don't know why she bothers asking for my opinion when she already knows what she wants to do, and *that's how it's going to be*. I feel like a servant, not a colleague."

From another: "I'm not happy at my current job, and after a lot of soul-searching, I've concluded essentially that while I may be in the wrong field, my BIG problem with my job is that I have a difficult boss. I think I might not have noticed so soon that I was probably in the wrong career if it weren't for the boss. Should I be looking to find a better job?"

A third stated: "I like my job but I can't stand my boss. He is always checking on me and I feel smothered. At times, he leads me to believe that I'm doing a good job, but later he comes back to me and tells me how terrible I am. What should I do? I just don't want to get abused like this anymore. He can be nice to me for periods, but he bashes my head in every few months. It's torture! I can't live life dreading work because of my boss, although I like what I do. I can't work like I am walking on eggshells."

And from one more: "I have a really shady boss. She pretends to be nice, but she does some really manipulative, underhanded things to get her projects done. Those things just seem incredibly dishonest to me. What should I do?"

My advice was offered through a story about a former client whom I had coached online. The person in question was a woman who had spent most of her life working for non-profit organizations and associations, but wanted to move to the business world. She had received several offers, and was particularly interested in a position at a major consulting firm. She believed it would give her the most solid business background to further advance her career . . . but she had a serious concern.

"My potential supervisor has a reputation as a screamer," she said. "When I was younger I might have been able to put up with that, but at this stage in my career, I don't think I can stand it."

I suggested that she discuss the subject with her potential boss before she turned down the opportunity. We rehearsed how to conduct the discussion. First, she would set a meeting with the prospective supervisor and start by stating reasons she liked the job and felt she could do it. Then, she would voice her concern and see how the boss would respond.

She did as planned. First, she reviewed the positives — what she liked about the job, and why. Then she said, "I have one concern, however. You've told me that, when you are under pressure, you may get excited and yell at staff. At this stage in my career, I don't believe I can work effectively under those conditions."

Her boss-to-be sat back in her chair, sighed and said, "I know, others have told me that. I don't mean to do it; it is something I am working on."

The potential supervisor then leaned forward and continued:

> Look. I can't guarantee that I won't ever yell at you, but I will tell you it is my intention to change that kind of behavior. I would like to have an agreement with you. If I ever yell, I want you to call me on it, and I want you to know that I'm open to discussing issues. I want to be a good and fair boss. Thank you for being willing to talk to me about this. I really would like you to join our team.

My client took the job. In the two years she worked in the company her boss never yelled at her. She reported that she and her boss,

> were under a lot of pressure quite a number of times on projects, but because we had held that discussion, we both learned how to communicate with each other, so that shouting in the workplace did not become a problem.

She added, "I am glad I had the conversation with her."

To all of you who have "bad" bosses: the key is communication. It is important that you start such conversations positively, but that at the proper time, you cite specific examples of "bad behavior." Most bosses don't want to be tyrants. They want to be respected, fair and effective. They may not realize what they are doing is offensive. They may be under pressure themselves.

Don't be a victim. Communicate. In most cases, adult-to-adult communication will improve an unpleasant workplace situation. It may not turn bad bosses into ideal ones, but it can go a long way toward making them tolerable.

If you have such a conversation and your boss stays in denial about his/her behavior and does nothing to try to improve the situation, it's time for you to make a decision about what you are going to do. Ultimately, *you* are responsible for your own career. Neither your boss nor your organization is responsible.

Life is too short to get ulcers because of a bad boss. If you have problems at work, do something about it. If you can't resolve it, consider going elsewhere.

Note to bosses: Do you see yourself in any of the above questions? If so, do something about it. Talk to others; get help if you need it. Being an abusive boss can block your own career growth, and can even lead to lawsuits, loss of productively, high turnover rates, a bad reputation among peers and superiors, and, in the worst case, quite possibly the loss of your own position.

Profiling a Great Boss

In the previous article, I responded to several questions about how to work with bad bosses — the ones who are inconsiderate and/or inconsistent. It is my observation, however, that bad bosses are the exception, not the rule. I am thus happy to share a letter I received from an employee who describes the qualities of a really terrific boss.

> Please permit me to summarize some of the skills my director has exemplified over the seven years we have worked together in two different associations, both of us with different job responsibilities.
>
> I learned early on that I could trust this man for support, encouragement, and dedication in sharing his own experience, knowledge and excitement about our profession. He counseled me to apply for my present position, and listened to my reasons for not wanting to take it. But he would not take no for an answer, and here I am!
>
> Now, what's so great about him?
>
> ➢ He always shares individual and team accomplishments, both publicly and privately.
>
> ➢ He encourages his staff to take risks.
>
> ➢ He communicates clear, consistent expectations and goals.
>
> ➢ He shares personal and professional experiences with a sense of humor and humanity.

- He encourages creativity in problem-solving and goal-setting.

- Recognizing unique skills and contributions of individuals and teams, he rewards his employees when appropriate.

- He addresses challenges immediately, and privately offers realistic, achievable solutions.

- Within and outside of the office, he supports and encourages the personal and professional development of each member of the staff.

- He won't tolerate gossip or demeaning discussions about our colleagues on the staff.

And perhaps best of all, my manager is fantastic because he makes me believe that I can be the kind of manager he is!

Those bosses who understand the essential difference between the old way of management by *ordering* people, and the new way of winning by *supporting* and *empowering* people, are the bosses who will be most successful. The boss mentioned earlier clearly falls into the latter category. Kudos to him for handling talent so effectively!

Too Close for Comfort: The Limits on Workplace Relationships

Not long ago I was contacted by a concerned employee who was distressed because an older female co-worker seemed intent on developing a much closer relationship with her than she wanted. She wrote:

> I am having a problem with a co-worker in my department. She is a very nice person, but she seems to spend more time in my office bothering me than in her office doing her job.
>
> When I first started this job, she took me under her wing and showed me the ropes. She pretty much became my mom on the job (she's twice my age). We've had lunch together, and I've even given her rides home. Now it seems that everywhere I go, there she is. She gets upset when I go to lunch with anyone other than her. On those occasions when I drive to work, she wants a ride home. She even wants us to start hanging out together on weekends.
>
> This is going too far for me. I've given my friend subtle hints to let her know that I don't have time to talk to her as much as she seems to want, but she doesn't seem to get it. I don't want to bring my boss into this because that might cause my co-worker to get into trouble.

As I noted to the writer of this letter, one of the most difficult things many of us ever have to do is to say "no" to someone, especially someone close to us. But it must be done occasionally if we are to communicate and collaborate effectively.

How do you say "no" to someone you care about? First, acknowledge the importance of the other person's request or position. Then tell the person why you can't or don't want to do what he or she has asked, and explain your reasons. Finally, suggest, discuss and attempt to work out an alternative that meets both of your needs.

I suggested to her that she invite her co-worker to have lunch together to discuss something important. Having lunch together would put her and her co-worker onto neutral ground in a public setting, but one where they likely would have enough privacy to carry on a meaningful discussion. I thought that she might begin by sayings something like, "I want to thank you for all the help you've given me in getting acclimated. Your advice and guidance have been very important to me. I also appreciate that you see our friendship positively."

To facilitate a dialogue where the conversation remains comfortable, she should pause briefly to gauge her co-worker's reaction. Then she could continue, "Lately, though, I feel you want us to spend as much time together as possible. Unfortunately, I feel pressure, since I need free time and weekends to do things on my own. I know you want to spend more time together, but I can't really do that and still get all the things done that I want to do."

Another pause would be appropriate at this point, with her listening attentively to any reaction. Her friend might suggest a solution that both parties could accept or discuss.

Absent such a suggestion, she could offer one herself. For example, "Why don't we plan to get together for lunch once or twice a month on a regular basis? And when our organization sponsors Spring Cleanup Day at the community house (or some similar work-sponsored activity), perhaps we could make arrangements to go together."

An approach along these lines would affirm the worth of her colleague; would assert her needs and desires while avoiding any criticism of the other person; and would offer a positive, gentle alternative to the co-worker's apparent design for increasingly close contact. A considerate, reasonable person should be able to accept this sort of approach without embarrassment or resentment.

Sexual Harassment Claims and Retaliation

Complaints about inappropriate personal, racy and intimate language and behavior in the workplace are, unfortunately, very common. It is bad enough when unwelcome language and actions of a sexual nature come from a co-worker, but it is far more offensive when it is perpetrated by a supervisor on a subordinate. Here's a typical complaint about a supervisor, as described in a letter I received from a correspondent:

> Our new executive director is doing some things that I would classify as sexual harassment. I am not the only one troubled or offended by his hand- and arm-kissing and public remarks. (These are only some of his objectionable behavior patterns.) But I think that if he got a complaint through our HR manager, he'd pretty easily figure out that it came from me, because I'm one of the more outspoken staff members.
>
> What protection would I have against reprisals he might take if I do complain, and my complaints become known to him? Do I have any right to talk to outside counsel? This situation needs to be addressed, but I'm not sure of my rights or how to proceed.

While I of course wanted to reassure her about her rights, my immediate reaction to her letter was to congratulate her for her determination to do something about the offensive conduct of her executive director, despite her concern that a protest might have negative consequences for her. I wrote her as follows:

> Brava! It's very heartening to learn that you've decided to explore ways to put a stop to an intolerable situation at your place of employment. While you may indeed

encounter some unpleasant moments if you speak out or take some concrete action, I'm quite sure that the results will be both gratifying to you and beneficial to all of those with whom you work, including (in the long run) your executive director himself.

As to her specific questions, I sought the views of two attorneys who have had considerable experience in the area of sexual harassment and other types of workplace discrimination. I do not provide legal advice, but my own experience, supported by the observations of the two lawyers mentioned, permit me to make some general comments which I believe may be useful to anyone concerned about sexual harassment:

A number of protections against sexual harassment are afforded by Title VII of the Civil Rights Act of 1964. The act not only defines "unlawful harassment," but also what constitutes "unlawful retaliation" by a manager or employer. Under Title VII, unlawful harassment can be verbal, visual, or physical. Harassment occurs when conduct unreasonably interferes with job performance or creates an intimidating, hostile, or offensive work environment. Under the Civil Rights Act, ethnic or religious slurs, racial or sexual jokes, and offensive sexual behavior or comments may be considered discrimination or harassment.

Title VII protects individuals who believe that they are being sexually harassed, and who speak out or take action to protest or correct the offensive behavior. Employees are protected against an employer's "unlawful retaliation," which is adverse action as a result of the employee's participation in a legally protected activity. Legally protected activity would include a formal or informal complaint about a supervisor's unwelcome touching and language. A supervisor against whom a complaint was filed would be taking a great risk if he were to retaliate against someone for having filed a complaint, and the employer-organization could be subject to serious liability if it were to countenance such retaliation.

Adverse actions include the following: threats to terminate employment; demotions, transfers, or actual termination of employment; negative performance evaluations; unfair criticism of work; sabotaging job performance; setting impossible work goals; derogatory remarks; unfair reprimands; and/or unwarranted disciplinary action.

It is advisable for an employee who wants to complain about harassment to begin by contacting his or her organization's human resources director, whose responsibilities normally include helping employees deal with the kind of issues you have mentioned. (Most human resources officials are used to handling sensitive matters with discretion.) In fact, an employee who wishes formally to seek redress for sexual harassment must seek relief through whatever procedures may be available in the employee's own organization, before he or she may bring an action in court.

Virtually all of the human resources officers (and other senior executives) I've known want their employees, individually or in groups, to disclose and protest harassing activity. Sexual harassment of employees is an embarrassment to organizations, and responsible managers want to prevent it, or, if it does occur, to stop it as quickly as possible.

It is now very common for employers to include, in their orientation programs for new employees, material on their organizations' policies concerning sexual harassment, and instructions to supervisors on how to prevent or stop it. That is welcome progress, and I hope that it encourages employees to speak out against sexual harassment so that every workplace is a comfortable one for everyone.

Changing a Light Bulb

Here is a short personal story that embodies one of those career lessons we all have to learn some time or another.

It starts with my dad, an active octogenarian. He cuts the lawn, trims the bushes, stains the deck, and is one of the first in line with a paintbrush or shovel on a community fix-up day.

So I was concerned one day when I called him and asked, "How are you doing?" and he responded, "Oh, not so good." He reported that he had to change a light bulb — the one in the ceiling in the hallway.

You can imagine what I must have thought: "Oh no! He's fallen off a ladder!"

"No, not that," he reported.

"Had he been shocked? Had he cut his hand?"

No, again. As it turned out, he wasn't injured in any way.

The light bulb had broken in the socket. Dad had to use pliers to twist the metallic part of the bulb out of the socket. But that didn't work too well, and he ended up twisting the entire socket and some plaster. Fixing the problem, and cleaning up, had taken him a good part of the day. Just to change a light bulb!

I sympathized with him, and then we laughed about it, because changing light bulbs is often what work and life seem to be about.

Since I told the story to some co-workers, it has become the mantra in the office when taking on a new project to ask, "Are we changing a light bulb here?"

How often do we decide to take on a project that, at least in the planning stage, looks like no big deal but turns into an organizational nightmare? Are you rolling your eyes right now with a sigh as you think of a specific project that recently drained you and your colleagues?

In the course of my own career, I've fashioned a number of sayings or maxims that serve as useful guides. One is, "Setting priorities means deciding what you're *not* going to do." Another one, which I call "Tom's Planning Rule," is "Whatever you plan, it'll take twice as long and cost three times as much."

I used to think that my maxims were hyperboles, but as I've read stories of cost and project overruns in big public projects and participated in my own light bulb-changing endeavors, I've come to realize that the double or triple planning factor is often not an exaggeration at all.

Maybe it would be a good idea before any of us agrees to take on some new project to ask, "Are we changing a light bulb here?"

Career Insurance

Here are some suggestions which I believe can, if taken together, form a sort of insurance policy for successful careers.

Take responsibility for your own career.
Don't count on others to make you successful, and don't blame others when you encounter bumps on your career path. You yourself determine where you are and what you are doing.

Conduct your own performance reviews.
Every six months, update your resume. Add the accomplishments you have made in your current job; any new skills you have gained during the period; awards or professional certifications you have received; and note any items of personal growth. If you find that you have nothing to add to your resume at this point, start planning what you are going to do so that six months from now you *will* have things to add.

Take an inventory of your work.
Make a pro's and con's list by drawing a line down the middle of a piece of paper. Put a "plus" on one side and a "minus" on the other. Write down what you do and don't like about your work.

Then jot down ideas that answer these questions:

- How can I do more of what I like?
- What can I change about what I don't like?
- Should I?
- Why?

Look inward:

- What is there?
- What do I *want* to be there?
- What do I need to change?

Diversify your sources of income.
People are living much longer and better now than at any time in history. 60 and 70 aren't "old" anymore; many of us will live into our eighties or nineties or even beyond. How are we going to afford such long lives? One way is by securing multiple sources of income.

Most of us have such multiple sources, or are in the process of developing them. These include the dual incomes of some couples; 401K, Keogh or IRA plans; dividends; interest; capital gains from savings and investments; a vacation home or cabin; equity in a house or condo; and earnings from part-time work as a consultant, writer or teacher. By diversifying your sources of income as you progress through your career, you create increased options for yourself, and you gain the peace of mind that comes with adequate income.

Follow your own path.
Life is not a dress rehearsal. If you don't fulfill that dream of yours now, when will you do it? Of course, you will achieve little unless you are willing to take risks. Calculate which risks are worth taking, and then take them. Remember that whether you like it or not, change will occur; you want to be the master of the changes that will affect you. To do that, try to focus on your goals, and keep moving toward them.

Respect the inner spirit of every individual.
I'm a consultant. By and large, I don't get to choose my clients. For more than 20 years, I have been working with people whom I had not previously met. People walk into my office, we

greet each other and then I become their career coach. I don't like them all, but I try hard to respect each person. Doing so makes my work a lot more pleasant and productive.

Listen to words. Listen for needs.
The willingness and ability to listen to what others have to say or suggest is a universally admired trait. It helps people gain acceptance, win promotions, and even get directions in a foreign county where they don't speak the language. The simple piece of advice, "Listen to words, listen for needs," was something I learned from an intern. I've never forgotten it; I try to apply it every day.

Ask for what you want.
This assumes you know what you want. Do you know what you want? To gain focus, write down your desires and goals. Outline a plan to meet them. Finally, add the names of people who may be able to help you with your plan of action. Once you have a clear idea of what you want, learn to describe it clearly, and don't be afraid to ask for it. If you don't ask for what you want, you may never get it.

Floss your teeth.
Weird advice? Not really. It's a shorthand way of saying that we have to take care of ourselves. That means developing healthy habits; tending to our relationships with the important people in our lives; and finding a good bit of our pleasure, personal growth and satisfaction outside the workplace.

Incidentally, it has been reported that people who floss their teeth regularly *do* tend to live longer and healthier lives than people who don't floss. Of course, that's probably due in large part to the fact that people who floss also do many other things which contribute to good physical health.

So: it is possible not only to live longer than those in previous generations, but also to have more healthy, active and productive lives than they did. *But ya gotta floss your teeth!*

The Effects of Technology

In the worlds of business, government and non-profit organizations, there is an increasingly common practice of reducing the number of administrative personnel and reassigning clerical tasks to professional staff people. As a result, many professional-level employees complain that they have less time than they should have to spend on programs and projects.

Like it or not, this seems to be the inevitable direction in which the world of work is moving rapidly. In the 1980's, the ratio of support staff to professionals in law firms was one-to-one. By the early 2000's, it had shifted to about one support staff for every 2.5 professionals. Now, it's moving quickly toward a 1:3, even a 1:4 ratio.[xii]

Quite simply, technology is changing the definition of "clerical tasks." In the days when most professional and business people sent formal messages in typewritten letters and memoranda, they needed lots of clerical support; that's no longer the case. Today, e-mail allows direct communication between parties without the need to produce or distribute paper documents. Voice mail allows for very rapid message exchanges. Both of these means of communication are commonly used by professionals themselves, without administrative support.

Another reason that the need for support staff is diminishing is the reduced need for middle managers to collect data from subordinates, "process" it, and pass it to superiors in summary form. Computer software now automates much of that work.

It may sound harsh, but my advice to professionals who are concerned by this trend is simply, "Get with the program."

Employers want workers who not only have valuable experience and good attitudes, but also have current skills and are comfortable and efficient in today's workplace.

SECTION III

Guidance for Human Resources Managers

The earlier an organization starts planning, the more lead time it will have to develop and implement creative options.

-Article page 131

RECRUITING AND RETENTION

Designing Your Interviews to Select Good Employees

Finding, attracting and hiring people who will get a given job done, or (better) will exceed the requirements of the job, can take effort. If you do it right, it's a sound investment. If you do it wrong, it's a waste of time, money and expectations.

Costs of a Bad Hire

- **The Same Time and Costs for a Good Hire PLUS:**
- **1-3 Month Poor Performance**
- **Time & Energy to Terminate**
- **Termination Paperwork**
- **Cost of Replacement Hire**
- **Internal Stress due to Turnovers and Unfilled Positions**
- **"Ripple Effect" of Bad Hires on Staff, Clients, Management**

But while a litany of advice is available for a job candidate on preparing for an interview, there's little advice for many managers on how to interview prospective employees. Managers need to know how to prepare for interviews, and what questions to ask, in order to compete successfully for talent in today's market.

If you are a manager, it will be important to take the time to make sure everyone involved in the hiring process is on the same page about his or her role in the process, about your firm's needs, and about the qualifications you are looking for in prospective employees. Remember that the best candidates get interviews with the best firms and organizations. And candidates know the difference between an employer who takes the hiring process seriously and one who treats it as an afterthought.

Assess and Define.

The first steps in preparing to interview a prospective employee are to assess your organization's needs, and to define the position which you want to fill those needs. Scan your organization and look for areas and skills that are missing or could be strengthened. Build positions around those missing or weak links. To define a position, identify the essential functions the job requires, and then determine the skills, knowledge and core competencies needed to perform those essential functions. If the position pre-existed, reflect on how other people did the job, especially what made them successful.

Select Interviewers.

Once you've established selection criteria, decide which other people will be involved in the interviewing and hiring process. You may want to include senior managers, managers of departments other than the one where the vacant (or new) position is located, employees who would be peers of your new hire, and even employees who would report to your new hire.

The recruiter and the hiring manager should interview finalists. The recruiter, the hiring manager *and at least two other individuals* should interview candidates for executive and supervisory positions.

Prepare the Interviewers.

Once you have selected appropriate people to assist you in conducting an interview, discuss selection strategy with them. Each interviewer should focus on certain key questions related to his or her personal expertise or background. Try to avoid asking a candidate repetitive questions. However, the same question phrased in different ways will often elicit somewhat different responses, which may be useful to you.

Carefully planned, well conducted multiple interviews will greatly increase the likelihood that you will hire the right candidate.

Recruit Candidates.

Plan your recruiting strategies. How can you attract the best possible candidates right from the start? You have several choices: print media such as newspapers, newsletters and trade publications; electronic media such as your organization's website and Internet job boards; advertising with professional associations; search and placement firms; job fairs; and networking through current and former staff colleagues, associations and personal contacts.

Don't overlook the last item just mentioned — recruiting through personal contacts. Many firms which have built staffs successfully have found that recruiting through their personal networks saves them time and money, and attracts qualified candidates. Some such firms offer referral bonuses to staff members, and/or retention bonuses to new hires in order to keep them on board.

In advertising a job, remember to portray your organization as a great place to work. Also describe the responsibilities of the job, candidates' requirements, and the methods candidates should use in responding.

Proceed Quickly.

Good candidates tend to have several options, and they lose interest if an organization delays or interrupts the hiring process or otherwise indicates that it does not have its act together. If the process unavoidably slows down once you've started it, keep your candidates informed. Make them aware of your timetable so they don't make negative assumptions about your level of interest in them.

Before you set up an interview, conduct a phone screening. This need be no more than a short conversation to confirm the candidate's contact information, check his or her interest in the position, and assess the candidate's fit with the company. Phone screenings save time because they enable you to weed out individuals who are no longer interested or don't seem like a good fit for your organization.

Keep in mind that there is a goodwill aspect to your initial contacts with a candidate, as well as a screening and selecting function. You want to impress the best-qualified candidates, but also to gain and maintain the respect of those whom you do not select.

Prepare for the interview.

First, consider the logistics. Make sure that your receptionist has the name of each candidate, knows how to pronounce it correctly, and greets the candidate personally upon arrival.

Have a comfortable, quiet place to conduct the interview. Have water on the table or desk for the candidate and yourself. If your office is small or cluttered, use another office or conference room. If this seems like a lot of effort, just think of how much more time and effort you'll spend later if you select someone who is not right for the job! Heed the adage, "There never seems to be time to do it right, but there's always time to do it over."

In preparing for the substance of an interview, first review the position requirements: the skills, knowledge and experience needed for the job. Review the candidate's resume and cover letter, if you have them. Note points which suggest a good fit between the candidate and the position, as well as indicators of a potential mismatch. Pay special attention to matters which seem to cause you concern, and plan interview questions related to those areas. Review requirements like good interpersonal skills and punctuality that are not mentioned in the job description but are implicit.

In order to analyze areas of potential match and mismatch, ask each candidate to describe past experiences that demonstrate application of skills, knowledge and competencies. Use open-ended questions like:

> "What is your greatest strength or ability?"
> "Why are you interested in this position?"

Remember to ask focused questions that concentrate on the candidate's experience:

> "What did you do in past positions?"
> "How did you do it?"
> "What were the results?"

Ask for specific examples so you do not receive vague answers.

Assemble a brief packet of information about your organization, and give it to the candidate at the end of the interview. This will only take a few minutes but it can facilitate future contacts and solidify a favorable impression. Finally, let the candidate know what the next steps are and when he or she can expect to hear from someone, then make sure someone in your organization follows through as promised.

Acquainting New Employees with Your Organization's Core Values

More than ever before, organizations of every kind are emphasizing "core values." These are both general (applicable to all institutions) and particular (tailored to the objectives, desires, cultures and needs of specific organizations).

In the first group are intangible qualities like courtesy, honesty, cooperativeness and respect. All employers rightly want all of their employees to have those values.

The second group consists of values which are determined by the circumstances of each individual enterprise. Every organization needs to identify its core values and integrate them into its daily business. If your organization has not done those things, it should start to do so as soon as possible.

The process of inculcating your core values into new hires needs to begin well before interviews. Whenever possible, these values should be mentioned in your position descriptions among the skills and behaviors required. Further, include mention of your core values in your recruiting materials, so that you attract applicants who identify with those values.

Successful organizations encourage their new employees to remain mindful of the organizations' core values, and continually coach and evaluate employees with regard to those values. If you are responsible for bringing new employees into your organization, you should place great importance on defining and teaching adherence to the core values of your enterprise.

Interviews

When interviewing potential new employees, try to elicit information about the candidates' values and abilities with regard to the skills and behaviors listed in the relevant position descriptions. When you interview for a position where particular values constitute essential functions, each interview should focus on those values. When discussing a given candidate with people whom the candidate has suggested as references, pay special attention to the matter of core values.

Orientation

Once you have recruited and hired people who demonstrate values that match those of your organization, focus their orientation on integrating the core values into their daily work. Publicize the values. Distribute information about your organization's core values at periodic meetings, and make sure that all employees remain aware of the nature and purpose of those values.

Supervisor's Meeting

At an early meeting with a new employee, his or her supervisor should review the organization's values to stress their importance. The supervisor should explain the organization's performance evaluation process, and discuss how the core values will impact evaluations.

Mentors

Assign a mentor to each new employee. The mentor should be a co-worker who can exemplify the organization's values and be willing to help the new employee integrate into the company.

Core Values

Finally, seek opportunities to reinforce your organization's core values, and to discuss their application in the daily life of the enterprise. That may be done in day-to-day work on projects, but also in staff meetings, performance evaluations and informal discussions. Finally, make sure that you notice, compliment and reward employees who demonstrate exceptional loyalty to your core values.

When a New Hire Doesn't Measure Up

Sometimes, despite the best efforts of both employer and new employee, their hopes and expectations are not met. Here is a letter from the head of a professional association describing such a case:

> After a three-month search for a new director of member services, we hired a person whom we thought would be ideal. When we interviewed him, he outlined an excellent plan for how he would increase services and build membership.
>
> Now, six weeks after the new hire came on board, I am having second thoughts about him. He has not started working on any of the proposed membership efforts he described in his interviews. Several other staff members have asked me anxiously when our new membership efforts will start to take shape.
>
> I want to make sure we give this new director the chance to do his job, and I'm not keen to do another search, but I am not sure he can handle the responsibility we've given him. Do you have any suggestions on how this situation can be salvaged? Any suggestions as to what we could have done differently in our hiring process?

When dealing with a new employee who is not living up to your expectations, try to initiate communication with the new hire right away. With any new employee, a supervisor should have at least a brief meeting every week throughout the first month, and then a meeting every other week, or monthly, for six months or a year. With new employees, you might even have a short exchange every day for a while.

Your meetings can consist of simply discussing positives and negatives for both your company and the new hire. Good starter questions might include:

- What is going well for you?
- What is not?
- What is going well for us?
- What is not?

There can be a more formal agenda as well, but it will be important to discuss informally both the positive and negative elements of the job situation, and to do so from the points of view of both the organization and the new employee.

As for designing a sound hiring process, you may want to consider the following suggestions:

- Define clearly the position for which you are hiring. State your expectations fully and carefully, setting out your organization's core values in the job description. Make sure
that those who will interview job applicants are well versed on the organization's needs and the job's requirements.

- Have several people interview each applicant; don't rely on just one person's judgment. For a position like Director of Member Services, it might even be appropriate to ask some association members to take part in the interview process. Coordinate among those participating so everyone does not ask the same questions.

- In each interview, ask behavior-based questions. Ask for examples of the applicant's responsibilities and accomplishments in previous positions. As you undoubtedly know, most savvy people in the world of associations could probably outline a fairly decent, or even a very good, member-services plan. But how many of them have ever developed and implemented such a plan?

- Finally, don't neglect to check references. Try to speak to former supervisors of the candidates, and to other individuals who know their personal and professional qualities.

Employment of People with Disabilities

Despite a decade of reforms mandated by the Americans with Disabilities Act (ADA), the unemployment rate of people with disabilities continues to hover right around 70%.[xiii] This is only a little better than the rates in the years just before the ADA was enacted.

Dr. Patience H. White is the founder of the Adolescent Employment Readiness Center (AERC), a group associated with Children's Hospital in Washington, DC, which prepares adolescents with disabilities for employment or post-high school education. Dr. White cites several studies that analyze the factors which seem to enable young people with disabilities to move successfully into adulthood. In an article titled "Transition to Adulthood," she wrote, "The factor most associated with successful outcomes was being involved as a youth with household chores."[xiv] Further, she added, "Successful persons also had a self-perception as *not handicapped*, and they had a network of friends, family and parental support without overprotectedness."

The studies cited by Dr. White make clear that when we exclude young people with disabilities from the sort of activities which young people normally engage in, and when we exempt youngsters with disabilities from duties which they could likely handle, we help predestine their underachievement.

Recently Morris Associates, Inc., worked with EXCEL!, an employment-focused organization of professionals with disabilities, in an effort to identify those things that facilitate or hinder the employment of people with disabilities. Morris Associates reviewed a great deal of the available research on this topic, and also conducted focus groups involving more than 20 employers in the Washington, DC, area. Throughout this process, two themes consistently emerged.

The first theme was that hiring people with disabilities must be strongly supported by the leaders of the hiring organizations. Both researchers and participants in our focus groups repeatedly cited "top management support," "strong corporate commitment," and "pro-active leadership" as the most important elements in any program to hire people with disabilities.

The second major facilitator is an organization's prior success in this area. Once an employer has had a positive experience working with people with disabilities, the employer is more likely to hire other disabled persons.

Not surprisingly, the converse is also true: little or no exposure to workers with disabilities produces managers and executives who are reluctant to hire such individuals. Managers who are not used to dealing with people with disabilities tend to have unrealistic and unnecessary fear of absenteeism, extra costs, and burdensome legal requirements or restrictions.

Providing employment opportunities for people with disabilities, and taking advantage of their talents, are not matters of concern only to disabled people; the issues concern all of us. Bringing people with disabilities into as much of the mainstream as they can handle well isn't just a "them" challenge, it's an "us" challenge.

I believe that as a nation, we should want to reduce the 70% rate of unemployment of persons with disabilities. After all, the history of our society is one of expanding opportunity, and it is consistent with our values to seek ways to help handicapped people to enjoy the opportunities that many of us take for granted.

Fortunately, that approach can serve hard-headed business interests, since the latent productivity in the pool of disabled persons is a resource of great potential value to individuals and the economy as a whole.

The ABC's of Relationships

Several years ago, I worked with the successful president of a small college in the Northeast. As president for 11 years, he had expanded a limited-degree college to one that offered a wide range of undergraduate degrees, and he had even established some graduate programs. One day we were discussing what makes employees, especially executives and professionals, successful.

"Do you know what my job is as president of the college?" he asked.

"What?" I asked.

He replied:

At the college, I work with a lot of bright, talented people. Some of them have eccentricities. Getting rid of them is not a solution. If I took that approach, I would have to spend time and money to replace them, and weeks or months adapting to the *new* employees' eccentricities. As president, I've learned that my job is to figure out what the employees' eccentricities are, and help them to get around them, over them, or through them so they can get their jobs done and be successful.

Clearly, the dynamics of the relationship between employee and employer depend on several issues, including management style, organizational culture, skills, abilities and expectations. A new employee may be the best assistant you have ever had, but he or she may be a disaster if placed in the culture of another organization.

What makes for a good or poor fit between employers and employees? As an outplacement consultant and executive coach, I've seen all the variations.

Relationships can be organized into three categories; I call them **A**, **B** and **C** relationships. One commonality in all types is that no one is solely responsible for the nature of a relationship; both people in the relationship determine its nature. In all of your relationships, there are three parts: you, the other person and the relationship itself. Often you'll find that a given employee, in different settings with different requirements and bosses, will perform differently. This **ABC** relationship guide is about the quality of relationships, not the individuals in them.

An "**A**" relationship occurs when the work environment and productivity tend consistently to meet or exceed the expectations of both the employer and the employee. This is the sign of a happy workplace.

Next are the "**B**" relationships, the ones that are "just okay" for both sides, wherein each individual receives enough of what he or she wants to make the relationship good, though not spectacular. They are often more than adequate but not usually superior. The employer and employee both get enough of what they need, and the relationship continues cordially and productively.

Not all employees are star performers, just as not all managers and executives are star performers. But many are good enough. They work out; they make enough of a contribution that they are worth keeping. In fact, these employees often form the foundations of their organizations.

The "**C**" relationships involve employees who simply don't work out, don't fit in and don't produce at the desired level.

Yet the employees in question often are quite capable and talented, which is why they were hired or promoted in the first place. Over time, however, the relationships maintained by the employees deteriorated and problems arose. In the past, some of our most prominent citizens have sometimes been involved in well publicized problems in employee relations. History and business are replete with examples: former Chrysler CEO Lee Iacocca and New York Yankees' principal owner George Steinbrenner come to mind.

The "C" relationships are those that are not working well for the employer, the employee or both. Your "C" relationships are the ones you talk about at home and when you're out with your friends. They are the employer-employee relationships that wear down both sides and occupy your thoughts away from your job. Something has to be done about these relationships. Change must happen.

The good news is that you can find an "A" relationship in some job — maybe not the one you're in now, but somewhere. Of course, you need to identify corporate cultures in which you will be able to work well.

Your attitude plays a large part in your ability to be half of an "A" relationship. Always try to maintain a positive attitude and learn to recognize which types of relationships you have with your colleagues and supervisors. Remember, successful and productive workplace relationships are key elements (and harbingers) of future success.

Retaining Valued Employees in a Competitive Environment

One of the questions most on the minds of good executives is this: "How can we keep our best employees from leaving to work elsewhere?"

A related, but frequently unspoken question is this one: "How can we keep our best employees from leaving to go to work *for our competitors?*"

Why Employees Leave

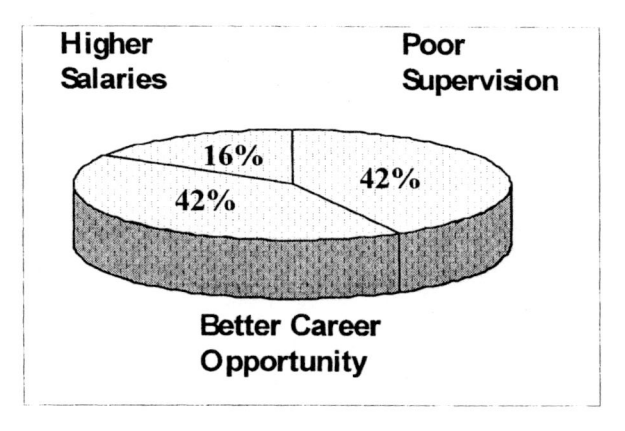

- Higher Salaries — 42%
- Poor Supervision — 42%
- Better Career Opportunity — 16%

Source: Saratoga Institute

That is not surprising, given the high cost of employee turnover. Replacing a departing employee costs a firm about 30% of the employee's annual salary, according to what the American Management Association (AMA) has called a "conservative" estimate.[xv]

Another survey, this one jointly commissioned by the Northern Virginia Technology Council and Virginia's Center for Innovative Technology, indicates that the cost of replacing an employee ranges from a low of $3,400 per hire to around 1.5 times the departing individual's salary.[xvi]

In 2000 and 2001, Morris Associates, Inc., participated in studies, led focus groups and produced a compilation of useful literature on the subject of best practices in recruiting and retention. Not surprisingly, these efforts concluded that attractive pay and benefits were important inducements to both recruiting and retention. But we also found that the retention of good employees depended in large part on the kind of recognition and career development given to them, and on positive, healthy work environments.

When asked, "What has your firm done to enhance retention?" there were many different responses. Here are some typical replies:

Attentive Listening.

"We meet with new employees to identify their likes and dislikes. We maintain an 'open door' policy so that new employees have easy access to the organization's executives."

Pleasant Environment.

"Our firm has causal dress days. We take pains to maintain a family-friendly environment. We allow quiet music in the workplace, and we try to accommodate any special needs of our employees."

Employee Recognition.

"Our managers host staff lunches, and recognize notable achievements with gifts presented publicly. We provide 'incentive awards' in the form of tickets to various events in the area."

Career Development.

One law firm said, "We try to develop career paths for all of our administrative assistants. We encourage our secretaries to be trained as legal secretaries, and we pay for the training. Where appropriate, we upgrade job titles. We reimburse employees for the cost of any work-related education or training which they complete successfully."

Enhanced Benefits.

"We look for ways to increase the attractiveness of the benefits we give our employees. For example, we pay our contribution into employees' 401K plans every 90 days or six months, instead of once a year. We give cash payouts for limited amounts of sick leave not used, and we provide cash awards for length of service. We have a program to reimburse transportation costs."

Emphasis on Wellness.

"Our organization tries to maintain a friendly, low-stress atmosphere which contributes to positive attitudes. We try to inculcate the value of leading a well balanced life. We cover all or part of the cost of health assessment programs, smoking cessation clinics and fitness club memberships."

The pillars of job satisfaction cited above are by no means unique to the world of law firms. The nursing profession, for example, seems to have similar values, as demonstrated by the results of a Nurse Recruiting and Retention Survey which Morris Associates conducted in conjunction with the Health Care Council for the National Capital Area. Survey respondents reported that nurses were most concerned with professional environments that recognize the importance of their work, and that value them as individuals; with opportunities for growth and professional advancement; and with management's ability to create a positive atmosphere in the workplace.

In our studies of law firm administrators, health care managers and others, we observed that the firms with the best track records in recruiting and retention were the ones which best identified what good employees want, and what motivates them to stay. Because those organizations also showed flexibility and willingness to make appropriate changes, they were able to enjoy the benefits which flow from hiring good employees and keeping them.

Layoffs and Reductions in Force

Alternatives to Downsizing

In recent years, many businesses and organizations have been hit by massive market changes. Most of them don't want to cut staff, even though they may be struggling to stay afloat. Often, they try cost-cutting measures like reducing non-urgent expenses, freezing salaries, adopting flextime schedules, and leaving vacated positions unfilled. Some organizations have been using pizza lunches for staff, and closing early on Fridays, to keep morale and productivity up.

Surveys indicate that downsizing usually decreases morale and productivity, and can cost firms more than they save. Firms which downsize must often cover the cost of severance pay and benefit distributions, the outsourcing of materials and services, and the hiring of consultants (who are sometimes former employees).

Smart companies and organizations have learned this lesson. They find ways to avoid or minimize the trauma and disruption caused by reductions in force and reorganizations.

Perhaps the most important thing an organization can do before cutting staff is to become focused and creative about restoring and increasing revenues. Organizations that concentrate on reducing outlays, rather than increasing income, may end up with disastrous results. Organizations which let people go may later have trouble rebuilding corporate culture, morale, productivity and effectiveness.

Management expert Peter Drucker has written that the best way to downsize an organization is to focus first on things that the organization does well — the areas that produce desired results.[xvii] Once those areas have been identified, Drucker suggests, the organization should invest more money, people, effort and thought in them. The organization should then look at all its other functions and decide whether it needs them at all. That is a much more efficient approach than simply cutting all functions across the board by a given percentage.

Robert M. Tomasko, author of *Downsizing: Reshaping the Organization for the Future*, highlights a four-step strategy to downsizing:

1. Build, don't destroy.
2. Use a scalpel, not a meat cleaver.
3. Keep the solution from becoming worse than the problem.
4. Stay lean.[xviii]

As noted above, downsizing can be expensive and traumatic for an organization. Wise managers therefore seek less drastic ways to reduce costs if that becomes necessary. Here are some steps which may be considered as alternatives to downsizing:

- Across-the-board pay reductions for a limited period of time.
- A 4-day or 4½-day workweek, every week or every other week.
- Having staff do work which is now contracted out.
- Job sharing.
- Marketing staff services to members of the organization, and to entities outside.
- Offering unpaid leaves of absence, or unpaid sabbaticals.
- A hiring freeze.
- A study of all operating costs to identify possible reductions.
- Consultation with the employees whose jobs are at stake, to see what alternatives they might suggest.

- Consultation with the directors and members of the organization.
- Retraining of existing staff to handle new work inside the organization, or to market the organization's services externally.
- Using video and teleconferencing for board and committee meetings, instead of paying for travel and lodging for meetings off-site.

A number of firms and organizations that have made early-out offers across the board have been stunned when far more people accepted the offers than they had anticipated, or when they lost people in key positions (this was especially painful in technology areas). Often, some of those who took advantage of early-out offers had to be rehired as consultants at high rates after they had received their severance packages!

Smart organizations evaluate their operations at least once or twice a year. They ask themselves, "What are we doing to increase revenues? What are the most effective and productive things we do now, and how can we enhance and expand those things?"

Finally, it is important that an organization not wait passively in hopes that finances will improve. The earlier an organization starts planning, the more lead time it will have to develop and implement creative options.

Managing a Downsizing

Many organizations have been forced to evolve due to rapid advances in technology, dramatic shifts in the types of goods and services they produce, and changes in the places of production. One of the realities of that evolution is that some businesses and other organizations will shrink, merge or disappear entirely. Handling such change in a creative way is perhaps the toughest challenge an executive will ever face.

Recently we were contacted by a conscientious human resources director of an industry association which was trying to cope with the fact that the industry it represented was consolidating. The dues paid by the association's member firms had dropped, and the organization's non-dues income had declined as well. The human resources director was being pressured by the association's board of directors to streamline. The association's president asked the human resources director to collaborate with the association's finance director in outlining a plan for downsizing, and the human resources director asked Morris Associates, Inc., for our ideas on how best to develop a sound downsizing plan.

We suggested that the human resources director try to persuade his superiors and colleagues that they should view the association's inevitable streamlining as an opportunity to build and grow, rather than as a demoralizing tragedy. Managers who concentrate on the negative will create a negative atmosphere and are likely to take actions that will result in decreased morale, lowered productivity and, all too often, increased expense. On the other hand, a well-planned downsizing which is presented in terms of possible future benefits is likely to soften a sense of loss, and gain the acceptance (or at least the acquiescence) of those affected by it.

While each plan has to be tailored to the unique situation it must address, here are some sound guidelines which we thought the organization might consider, and which have broad applicability:

Analyze your organization's core competencies, and strategize around them.

Determine which areas of your association or company yield positive results for your stakeholders. Distinguish between activities with high and low values in terms of your organization's mission. When you have identified the most productive aspects of your operation, design a plan to build on those core strengths. Then shape your organization to fit the strategy.

In so doing, you will need to reinforce and multiply the activities that produce the best results. That may require that you re-allocate resources, but it is wise to seek alternatives to terminating employees if at all possible.

Explain what you are doing, and why, to the people who will be affected.

The three groups affected by a downsizing are those who go, those who stay and those who deliver the news. That is everyone! Therefore, everyone in the organization needs and deserves timely information about the purpose and progress of a downsizing.

Communication is a two-way process. As an organization begins to think about a possible downsizing, it should also consider getting in touch with a good outplacement firm. An organization must have a plan for each phase of a reduction in force (RIF), and an outplacement firm can provide ideas and checklists to outline and strategize the termination process. An outplacement firm can provide valuable services to help an organization plan for a downsizing, and can help the affected employees cope with it.

There are many fine outplacement firms, but I am naturally partial to Morris Associates, Inc. Our website is :

www.morrisdc.com.

If you have to select certain functions to reduce, use a rifle, not a shotgun.

When you identify activities that produce the greatest results for your members, also evaluate all *other* functions to determine whether all of them are really needed. For each one found to be necessary, ask, "Can this function be performed differently at a lower overall cost?"

Be prepared for additional costs.

A reduction in force costs money at first and saves money later, if at all. In addition to the cost and effort involved in administering the RIF itself, an organization which is downsizing has to take into account severance pay, the continuation of insurance coverage, pay for unused vacation time, transition assistance and several other items.

All of these expenses need to be calculated carefully. Severance pay, usually worth from one week's to one month's salary for each year of service, is often given to those who lose their jobs. In addition to length of employment, other factors that must be considered with regard to severance pay for a given employee are the employee's position in the organization, the organization's financial situation, and whatever factors may be unique to the organization and its industry.

Implement the plan, move ahead, and watch the bottom line.

A downsizing plan should be constructed from the head *and* heart. In that process, managers must aim for productivity gains and financial results that will help protect the organization from further reductions. Managers will increase their chances of success if they follow these basic rules of downsizing:

> ➢ *Don't make cuts across the board.*
> ➢ *Reshape, don't decimate.*
> ➢ *Communicate early to those who will be affected, and*
> ➢ *Plan what to do after the downsizing.*

Managers must be careful to address the needs of those who go, those who stay, and those who have to oversee the transition. That is the best way to protect morale and productivity so as to prepare the downsized organization for a smooth future.

SECTION IV

Guidance for Career Coaches

*In today's workplace, people
are looking for a style of leadership that
includes integrity, an inspiring vision and a
compelling business strategy.*

-Article page 149

Career Assessment: Many Approaches

There are many exercises which can help people clarify their desires, interests and abilities with regard to work. These exercises are commonly known as "career assessments." Carrying out a career assessment can be a lot like making chili: there are many ways to do it, and many produce fine results, but what makes the best chili *for you* is using a variety of ingredients in a combination that is right *for you*.

In the same vein, successful people are those who do what they like to do, and what they do well. A successful career assessment will help you figure out what you like to do, what you do well, and how you can integrate those things into an income-producing career.

Virtually all career development books stress self-assessment and setting personal objectives as first steps. In an assessment, you are answering four questions:

- ➢ What do I want to do?
- ➢ Where do I want to do it?
- ➢ How do I want to do it? and
- ➢ What do I want to get in return?

There are scores of standardized "self-assessment" instruments, but none can tell you what you should do or who you should be. The tests do not assess people; instead they assess attributes like skills, abilities, competencies, values, personality, communication style and interests. In turn, these attributes need to be separated into categories that can be measured by an assessment instrument.

Discuss career goals with colleagues, friends and family. Such conversations could also profitably cover strengths, weaknesses, values and preferred work environments.

This informal discussion method can be useful, but it is subjective and incomplete. The information you get from your discussions will be shaped by how sincerely you ask the questions, how honestly you listen to the answers, and whom you choose to ask in the first place. Many people have limited experience in the world of work, so their observations and recommendations may be narrow. Also, be aware that some colleagues may feel threatened at the prospect that you might advance while they stay put.

Of course, input from people who know you and care about your success is almost always a good idea, especially when combined with other assessment information.

Contact and speak with people who work in the new areas you are considering. Make sure they understand you are looking for information, not necessarily a job, when you approach them. You might try getting involved in new areas in your current workplace to get experience in and a feel for the kind of work you are considering.

There are dozens of written exercises for job seekers; many job-change and career-development books contain exercises. Exercises in career-development books often ask you to list and explore past successes, ideal jobs, "perfect days" and preferred future environments. Exercises that focus on such "positives" provide great places to start.

What Color Is Your Parachute?, by Richard Nelson Bolles, is a classic work for job seekers, and it's loaded with helpful written assessment exercises.[xix]

There are also well established self-assessment instruments, many of which require the help of someone certified to interpret the instruments. The experience and insight of a trained and experienced professional may be required for self-assessments to be useful and applicable to given individuals. Assessment tools can be tremendously informative, especially if combined with other assessment methods and discussed with someone who understands the capabilities and limitations of those instruments.

The Campbell Interest and Skill Survey (CISS) is an example of a comprehensive assessment tool which could be used to identify your interests and skills. It compares your results to the results of successful people in the fields you're interested in. The CISS can indicate which fields are compatible with your interests and skills. With the help of a certified counselor to interpret it, your CISS will offer you guidance regarding professions that you may enjoy.

As you get more focused about what you want to do and where you want to do it, begin visualizing yourself successfully finding and doing that work. Set objectives and write out a plan of action on how you will reach your goals. Successful people have a destination in mind, and a plan for getting there.

Writing a resume that focuses on where you want to go, what you want to do, and what you can offer to others is a good way to determine whether your assessment process has been beneficial.

Take the "quick test." Can you summarize what you want to do on an index card? If not, you need to do more work or get more help to become focused.

Advice from Successful Job Seekers

Here's some practical advice I received from two successful job seekers. Both individuals are human resources executives who had just completed successful transitions to new positions.

The first drew five key conclusions about what made his search successful. He wrote:

1. **Networking:** I established a broad network over the years, and referrals from people in my network helped me get in the door at my current place of employment. I'll make sure to keep my network going; I don't underestimate the range and effectiveness of networking.

2. **Communication:** I kept others informed of my progress. My network does care, so I've made it a point to keep everyone apprised of my efforts.

3. **Accepting help:** People truly wanted to assist me, and I allowed them to do so. I sought their opinions, leads and introductions. The results were helpful connections and good ideas.

4. **Personal time:** I forced myself to take time to recharge. The time spent with my family was great.

5. **Positive attitude:** This can't be emphasized enough. It was often tough for me to keep up the smiles and the happy face, but my positive attitude was noticed and appreciated by others.

He added another piece of advice for job seekers, and he showed by his behavior that he took his own advice. "Everyday," he said, "I got up, got dressed and got moving."

The second human resources executive shared with me her view that despite the many great things an outplacement firm can provide, there are some things that only the person seeking to change careers can provide for himself or herself. She mentioned a sense of identity; motivation and desire to do the work; self-management, patience and discipline; and a willingness to ask for and accept help.

She also emphasized that job seekers should keep in mind the Rule of Three P's:

Purpose: Have a purpose for what you're doing; don't just use a scattershot approach. Have a plan and follow it.

Persistence: Don't give up! The process can be hard on the ego, but stick with it.

Patience: All good things come in good time.

How to Avoid Being De-selected

By and large, hiring is a selecting-out process more than a selecting-in process. For every one person hired, many other candidates usually are selected out. A key to being selected in is to avoid being selected out. Sadly, most of those who are de-selected are themselves largely responsible for their fate: their own missteps have cost them dearly.

Here are ten pitfalls to avoid in the job-search process:

1. Negative attitude. Negative self-talk generates negative results. "Nobody will hire me because of my age, gender, race, etc." "I can't do . . ." "I haven't ever . . ." This sort of self-defeating thought becomes a self-fulfilling prophecy. You may think you won't say those things in an interview, but what's in your head does get communicated — if not in words, then in tone and body language.

2. Unclear focus. You will likely make a poor impression in an interview or during networking if you don't know what you're good at, can't present your skills effectively, or don't know what job or industry interests you. To avoid that, take whatever time is necessary to clarify what you need, what you're seeking and what experiences you can build upon. Develop the skill of talking about your strengths and giving examples of things you have done that reflect those strengths. Practice until your presentation is focused, clear, and reflects who you are.

3. A past-directed resume. The problem with most resumes is that they are obituaries. You need a future-directed resume that quickly gives readers an idea of your talents and what you can offer employers. Your resume represents your bridge to your future, so focus it on the things you want to do rather than the things you have done. Point your resume in the direction you want to go.

A resume must look clean, clear and inviting. The printed version must be on quality paper. If you are faxing a resume, make sure the text is clear and crisp. If you are e-mailing it, test for format quirks. Make sure that it is easy for the recipient to copy, scan and print your resume. Also, check for typographical and grammatical errors.

4. **Unfocused cover letter.** A well crafted cover letter is perhaps more important than your resume. Tailor your cover letter to the relevant position and organization by giving examples of how your skills, experience and past accomplishments relate to the responsibilities and requirements of the position. Use a standard business-letter format with the correct name and title of the recipient. Reference the position, and tell the recipient why you'd make a good fit. Say, "Thank you." State how you will follow up. Include your contact information.

5. **Limited search.** Too many people select themselves out of consideration by only responding to ads and not expanding on the contacts available to them. Use your phone, fax, e-mail and "snail" mail to let people know what you are looking for. Ask for referrals. Use newspapers, the Internet, professional journals, associations, educational and community affiliations and libraries to identify leads and contacts. Keep in contact with your network after your search is complete.

6. **Negative networking.** Networking is not about asking who is hiring. It's about information and referrals. Talk with your family, friends, colleagues, fellow alumni and association members. Reconnect with people you've known in the past. Any community is a source of networking opportunities. Ask your contacts to give you ideas, suggestions, information and feedback . . . and pay attention to what they tell you.

7. **Not preparing.** Most people do not have a lot of experience with job interviews. You may even be experienced in interviewing job applicants, but that doesn't necessarily mean that you'll be an expert on the other side of the interview table. Learn as much as

possible about the organization, industry, department and position you are interested in as well as the people who will be interviewing you. Prepare thoughtful questions and try to anticipate, and be ready to answer, questions which you will be asked. Develop a positive vision for how you want the interview to go.

8. Not listening. Avoid the "sell yourself" mindset. Focus your discussion on the firm and the position you're interested in rather than on yourself. Ask questions and listen carefully to the answers; pay careful attention to your interviewers' questions, and make sure to answer them. If you're in doubt as to your answer, ask, "Does that answer your question?" In all of that, try to find out what the interviewer and his/her firm are looking for, and then match your skills and abilities to their needs.

9. Failure to follow up. Don't take the "If they wanted me, they would have called me," attitude; be captain of your own ship. Send thank-you notes after every interview or network meeting, and send follow-up letters when appropriate.

10. Leading an unbalanced life. Keep in mind all your roles as a person, and continue doing things in all the important parts of your life.

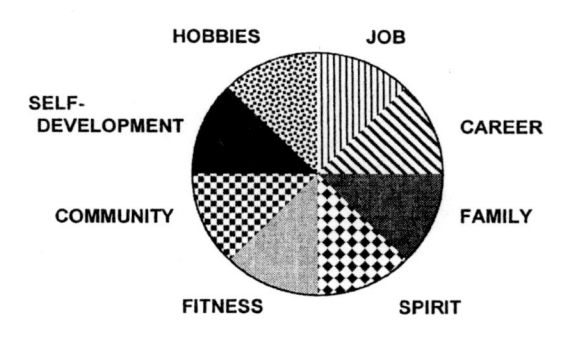

It might be useful to review the foregoing paragraphs periodically during your job search. Remember: don't de-select yourself by making the wrong moves!

Career Management and Quality of Life

One of the great benefits of professional associations is their ability to provide useful information on broad issues relating to the industries they represent. One such organization is the Association of Career Professionals International (ACP).

In 2001, ACP's Future Focus Committee, composed of career management specialists from many countries, issued a report on "Trends and Issues Affecting Career Management."[xx]

The report noted major trends relating to changes in the world of work and the quality of life. Here are some of the key findings about today's typical workplace environment:

- In the "information age" workplace, two challenging factors, rapidity and complexity, are coming together. People are being asked to work at a faster pace within increasingly complex situations.

- People must now work more quickly in a more complex workplace and market environment. More work is being done faster and sometimes with fewer people. It is becoming more and more difficult for people to keep up with the flow and complexity of information. There is a greater need for a rational, analytical approach to organizational issues, which forces people to use higher levels of thinking.

- People are challenged to think independently, yet work as a team.

- In today's workplace, people are looking for a style of leadership that includes integrity, an inspiring vision and a compelling business strategy.

The second major trend highlighted in ACP's report was the emergence of "quality of life" issues. Highlights:

- Many people are assessing the way they use their time and energy. They want a better balance between their work lives and personal lives.

- More workers leave jobs in search of a simpler and more fulfilling way of life. Many are looking for different options including self-employment, more relaxed work environments, or flexible situations.

According to the report, successful employees in today's workplace:

- Understand the current dynamics of jobs and careers, not merely what jobs and careers *used to be* like.

- Quickly learn new work roles, beyond the roles they played in their former jobs.

- Understand and accept new organizational structures.

- Quickly become familiar with new structures of the workplace.

- Assume positive new attitudes and views of jobs and careers.

What *skills* are necessary for successful employment? The report found that "both technical and interpersonal skills will be required."

What *attitudes* will be necessary for successful employment? "Being open to change, being able to manage ambiguity, being willing to multi-task and being more self-directed and self-managing."

Personal contact continues to be the key to managing the dramatic changes which are taking place in the world of employment. As ACP's report noted, despite the many technological advancements that have been made over the past quarter century, "making connections with individuals still remains the number one technique for getting back to work or shifting how and where work is done."

A Workshop on the Employment of People with Disabilities

-Written with Dr. Robert S. Rudney

As noted in an earlier section of this book, while the Americans with Disabilities Act of 1990 (ADA) has been a boon to people with disabilities in term of access to public accommodations and services, it seems to have had less notable success in expanding employment opportunities for the handicapped. The EXCEL! Networking Group seeks to develop strategies and techniques to expand employment opportunities for people with disabilities.

A few years ago, EXCEL! partnered with Morris Associates, Inc., to sponsor a 3-day intensive work-search training program for EXCEL! members. By the conclusion of the workshop, participants had developed a consensus that similar programs could be highly useful to other organizations in planning work-search programs for people with disabilities. In fact, many participants said that although the program was designed originally for individuals with disabilities, it could easily be adapted to assist virtually anyone seeking new employment.

The Morris Associates/EXCEL! workshop was planned for college-graduate job seekers with disabilities who already had some work experience. The impairments of the participants varied widely, as did their ages and work experiences. Some of the participants were attempting career transitions, while others were seeking to re-enter the labor force after years of unemployment.

Summarized below are the key strategies which evolved during the workshop. The strategies indicate appropriate attitudes and baseline plans for workshop organizers and participants.

Strategy 1: Take responsibility for yourself.

Individual initiative is essential for obtaining employment in today's competitive environment. A mentality of dependency and passivity, sometimes nurtured by well- meaning rehabilitation counselors, seldom yields results.

A mantra of the Morris/EXCEL! workshop was *"Show how, but don't do for."* The principle behind the mantra was that a good workshop program should provide participants with necessary tools and strategies to undertake a successful job search, but should also foster an understanding that the search itself is the responsibility of each participant.

This attitude led participants to make considerable efforts to building group solidarity. Those who caught on quickly helped those who had difficulty, and participants with visual or oral impairments were helped by those who did not have those types of disabilities. (The personal bonds between such participants were strengthened during subsequent group-support meetings.)

Strategy 2: Do not highlight disabilities during the workshop.

Workshop participants learned to address disabilities only as they should be addressed during a job search, which is to say only to the extent that a disability relates to job performance.

During the workshop there was no practice of catering to participants' disabilities. If a participant had difficulty understanding a point or completing an assignment, the necessary adjustments were made on the spot. On some occasions when a participant needed help, the flow of the workshop discussions went on without interruption, as other participants were able to assist individuals in overcoming particular challenges.

Unlike other programs for people with disabilities, the workshop did not focus from the start on a recitation of ADA rights and guidelines. Had the workshop focused on the ADA at an early stage, some participants might have been encouraged to conclude that they had unique rights and special privileges, while other participants may have come to feel that they were outside the mainstream of the workforce. The workshop sidestepped such problems by focusing on the key objective of any successful job search: matching a candidate's abilities with a potential employer's needs, in order to demonstrate that the candidate is well qualified for the position regardless of his or her disability.

Strategy 3: Emphasize positive, creative thinking.

The workshop encouraged participants to think outside the box. Some people with disabilities tend to think narrowly and focus on just one or two occupations in which, they believe, they are capable of performing well. The workshop sought to broaden horizons, since people who fixate on their limitations tend to develop a negative, self-defeating mindset.

The Morris/EXCEL! workshop emphasized the need for each job seeker to be versatile, to maximize potentialities and to keep an open mind. Every participant completed a self-assessment designed to broaden his or her career search by presenting a range of possible interests and skills to prospective employers.

Strategy 4: An individual's resume should show work done in the past, even if the person can't do it now.

Several participants had disabilities due to traumatic illnesses or accidents. In some cases the impairments made it impossible for the people in question to work at the same levels as they could earlier in their careers. Should the resume of someone in that situation list only the person's current capabilities, or should it also include previous work?

Workshop participants agreed that the latter approach was a valid one for the resumes of persons with adult-onset disabilities. While recognizing that there might be a need to disclose a disability relatively early in the application process, participants also thought it was better to present their fuller capabilities and experience on resumes. Such an approach would also give a candidate the opportunity to highlight the strong personal qualities demanded for recovery and rehabilitation, thus turning a potential negative into a positive. After all, recovery and rehabilitation often require the same sort of personal characteristics as successful work performance: persistence, courage, flexibility, adaptability, sensitivity to others, the ability to overcome obstacles and avoid frustration, and so on.

Strategy 5: Address employers' concerns regarding accommodation.

Very often, when an interviewer meets with a job applicant who has a disability, the interviewer wonders whether his or her organization will be able to accommodate the candidate. Such concerns cannot be ignored, since the issue of accommodation may become central to the employment decision (even though the employer may be reluctant to admit it). Normally, the concern does not reflect prejudice against people with impairments, but rather a desire to ensure that the candidate can actually perform the duties of the position, and that the accommodation required can be accomplished without excessive cost. Workshop participants felt that a candidate with a disability should help an interviewer address those uncertainties squarely.

It may be desirable, therefore, for a candidate being interviewed to initiate and lead discussion of whatever accommodation the candidate believes will be required for him or her to perform the duties of the position satisfactorily. That approach can be reassuring to an interviewer, even though it may not be legally necessary. (Normally, an *interviewer* may raise the issue of accommodation only after an offer of employment has been made; and a *candidate* has no obligation to disclose information regarding his or her disability, but only about the sort of accommodation that will be needed.)

In the Morris/EXCEL! workshop, participants had an animated discussion about strategies that persons with disabilities could employ to place potential employers at ease. The consensus of the participants and leaders was that if the job candidate takes the initiative in talking about necessary accommodation, and if he or she can inject an element of humor into the discussion, the prospective employer is likely to overcome any reluctance to consider appropriate accommodation. In the interview process, the candidate needs to demonstrate that he or she is comfortable with his or her disability, and that other people should feel the same way. This approach helps focus the interviewer on the qualifications, rather than the limitations, of the candidate.

One workshop participant described his approach to overcoming the accommodation concern by cheerfully telling the potential employer that all he needed, "was a place to sit and a place to put my walker." A woman in a wheelchair tells potential employers, "the only accommodation I need to work here is a string to pull the ladies' room door closed behind me and I have the string right here." An executive who lost his right arm extends his left for a handshake and says with a smile, "In my business, I've learned to be a switch-hitter."

Strategy 6: Bring role models into the workshop.

A workshop discussion of the disclosure and accommodation of disabilities may often be facilitated by role models — people with disabilities who have been successful in their own careers. The Morris/EXCEL! workshop drew upon the expertise of a human resources executive who is an amputee. The executive was able to provide a fresh perspective, particularly during the interview exercises, on disclosure and accommodation issues.

In a follow-up review session, workshop participants heard from another successful executive with a disability, the Vice President of Human Resources of several nationally-known hospitals. Participants were grateful for the practical tips from this expert on the topic of what employers are looking for in candidates.

Strategy 7: Record Conclusions and Recommendations.

Participants in the Morris/EXCEL! workshop reached consensus on four recommendations for people with disabilities who are looking for employment:

Recommendation 1: People with disabilities have to make public and private agencies more responsive to their employment needs.

Recommendation 2: People with disabilities should take the initiative to create their own organizations to represent their views and to develop programs that respond to their needs.

Recommendation 3: Individuals with or without disabilities need to take responsibility for their own personal growth and development in order to be competitive in today's market.

Recommendation 4: The ADA has provided a more level playing field in terms of physical access to facilities, and initial consideration for employment. However, people with disabilities must be pro-active on their own behalf if they are to be successful in today's professional world.

Endnotes

[i] Joe Carrieri. *Joe DiMaggio: The Promise.* Carlyn Publications, 2000.
[ii] *Webster's II New College Dictionary.* Boston: Houghton Mifflin Company, 1995.
[iii] *Webster's II New College Dictionary.* Boston: Houghton Mifflin Company, 1995.
[iv] Vic Elford. *Porsche High-Performance Driving Handbook.* Osceola: Motorbooks International, 1994.
[v] Bob Bondurant. *Bob Bondurant on High Performance Driving.* Osceola: Motorbooks International, 2000.
[vi] Stephen Covey, management lecture given at the Woodley Park Marriot, Washington, DC, 1996.
[vii] Figures from the Census Bureau and Bureau of Labor Statistics.
[viii] Mark S. Granovetter. *Getting A Job: A Study of Contacts and Careers.* Cambridge: Harvard University Press, 1979.
[ix] Alexis De Tocqueville. *Democracy in America.* Cambridge: Sever and Francis, 1862.
[x] Kimberly N. Hunt, ed. *Encyclopedia of Associations.* 42nd Edition, Three Volume Set. Farmington Hills: Gale Group, 2005.
[xi] C. Colgate, Jr. and John J. Russell, ed. *National Trade and Professional Associations of the United States Director,.* 17th Edition. Washington: Columbia Books, 2004.
[xii] From personal conversations with law firm administrators.
[xiii] Andrew J. Houtenville and Richard V. Burkhauser. "Did the Employment of People with Disabilities Decline in the 1990s, and Was the ADA Responsible?" *Cornell University Employment and Disability Institute Research Brief.* August 2004.
[xiv] Dr. Patience White. Children's Hospital Newsletter. Washington, DC.
[xv] American Management Association International, 1601 Broadway, New York, NY 10019.
[xvi] Northern Virginia Technology Council and Virginia's Center for Innovative Technology report, 2000.
[xvii] Peter Drucker. "The Right Way to Downsize," *Executive Update.* April 1999.
[xviii] Robert M. Tomasko. *Downsizing: Reshaping the Corporation for the Future.* New York: Amacom Books, 1987.
[xix] Richard Nelson Bolles. *What Color Is Your Parachute?: A Practical Manual for Job-Hunters and Career-Changers.* Berkeley: Ten Speed Press, 2004.
[xx] Association of Career Professionals International, Fourth Report on Trends and Issues Affecting Career Management, 2001.

INDEX

A

Accommodations
(reasonable), 155-156
Administrative personnel, 56
57, 106-107, 129
resume openings for, 41
Age, 19, 46-47, 145
American College Advisory
Service, 49
American Management
Association, 127
Americans with Disabilities
Act, 121, 152-158
Assessment (career), 28-34, 35,
40, 43, 53, 129, 140-142, 154
questions, 102-103, 140
what is assessed, 140
Associations,
consolidating industry, 134
finding a job through,
71-73
Attire, 22-23, 128, 143
Attitude,
positive, 19-24, 28-30, 61,
63, 74, 107, 126, 129, 143,
150, 153

B

Bosses, 57, 125
difficult, 88-91
qualities of great, 92-93

C

Campbell Interests
and Skill Survey, 142
Candidates,
how to recruit, 110-114
Career,
changer, 19, 28, 33-34, 37,
51, 58, 62-63, 71
coaching, 19, 43, 51, 63,
104, 125, 142
goals, 21, 27, 29, 48-49,
51, 55, 62, 71, 85, 103, 104,
140, 142
tips for success, 102-105
Choosing between jobs,
33-34, 84-85
Cloning Yourself, 28
Communications, 23, 75,
88-91, 94, 106, 118, 135, 140
Compensation, 80-83
Core competencies,
an organization's, 135
Core values,
communicating them,
115-117, 119
Cost of replacing
employees, 127-130
Cover letters, 44, 45, 46, 49,
114, 146
Creative thinking, 154

D

Degrees,
 credibility without, 48-49
De-selection,
 avoiding, 145-148
Disabilities, people with,
 accommodations
  needed, 157
 adult onset (and
  resumes), 155
 assessment for, 28-29
 disclosure of ,157
 employing, 121-123
 resumes for, 153-155
 strategies for job seeking,
  152-158
Downsizing,
 alternatives to, 132-133
 general, 24, 26, 27
 managing, 134-137
 rules for, 137
 strategy, 132
 surviving, 61-63
Dress (see attire)

E

Employees,
 eccentricities, 124
 reasons they leave, 127
 retaining valued, 127-130
Employees (new),
 problems with, 118-120
 questions for, 119
 selecting, 110-114
Employment gaps, 40-42

Employment opportunities
 for people with
 disabilities, 152
Encyclopedia of Associations,
 71-72
Excel! Networking Group,
 28-29, 121, 152-157
Eye contact, 23, 76

F

*Factoring Your Past
 Accomplishments* (exercise),
 28

G

Government,
 resumes for, 54
 transition from, 53-56
Group interviews, 76

H

Haldane, Dr. Bernard, 28
Hire,
 costs of a bad, 110
Hiring process,
 designing a, 110-114,
  119-120
Human resources,
 skills of, 50-51
 transitioning from, 50-52

I

Image, 22-23, 69
 of self, 19-21

Impairments,
  visual or oral, 153
Income,
  diversifying, 103
Interviews (employers),
  core values, 115-116
  for good employees,
    110-114, 119
  group, 76
Interviews (job seekers),
  64-69, 84
  degreeless, 49
  disabilities, 155-157
  dress, 22
  focus, 145
  group, 75-76
  listening during, 147
  matching needs, 84
  negative attitude, 145
  panels, 74, 76
  phone, 74-75
  preparing for, 146-147, 80
  questions to ask, 66-67

J

Job,
  dissatisfaction with,
    31-32
Job search,
  advice for, 133-134
  and associations, 71-73
  disabilities, 153-158
  during holidays, 59-60
  methods, 65

Job seekers with disabilities,
  152
  style and relationships,
    124-125
  supporting people
    with disabilities, 122

L

Lateral moves,
  in job, 33-34, 57
Law firms,
  technology in, 106-107
Layoffs,
  alternatives, 131-133
  plans if leaving, 62
  signs of, 61
  vision during, 24-25
Leads,
  finding, 60, 143, 146
Life,
  quality of, 149-151
Listening,
  with impressions, 23

M

Management,
  creating a positive
    atmosphere, 130
  degree, 48
  downsizing, 24, 26, 131-137
  employee recognition, 128
  holidays, 59
  insecurity, 64
  interview, 110-114
  interview questions to ask,
    67

Management (continued),
  interview training, 68
  lateral moves, 33
  moving up, 57
  of staff, 92, 93
  qualities of good, 93
  resume preferences of, 55
  sexual harassment, 97-99
  skills for resumes, 50-51
Mental image, 19-25, 29, 61

N

National Trade and Prof. Assoc. of US Directory, 71
Negative attitude, 19-20, 24, 27, 46, 134, 145, 154
Negotiating,
  for job, 69, 80-83
  negotiable perks, 82
  within job, 34
Networking, 64-70, 71, 72, 84, 143, 145, 146, 147
  building a network, 31
  communicating skills, 46
  questions to ask, 66-67
  to find employees, 112
  where to do it, 70
  with disabilities, 121
No,
  how to say it, 94-95
Northern Virginia Technology Council, cost of
    replacing an employee, 127-128
Nurses,
  recruiting and retention, 129

O

Offers,
  attitude, 68
  change within job, 33
  deciding between, 85
  discussing disabilities, 156
  early-out, 133
  job, 64, 69, 73, 79, 80, 82, 84-85, 89
Outplacement, 125, 135, 136, 144, (also see Downsizing, Layoff, Reduction in Force)

P

Positive (creative) thinking, 154
Positive mental attitude, 19-24, 28-30, 61, 63, 74, 107, 126, 129, 143, 150, 153
Personal characteristics, 155
Pro-active (on your own behalf), 158

Q

Qualifications (employees),
  candidates, 112-113
  indicating, 48
  of people with disabilities, 156
  rather than limitations, 156
  too qualified, 46-47
Qualifications (employers),
  attracting qualified candidates, 112-113
  sought in an employee, 110

R

Recruiting, 110-114, 116, 128-130
  describing in a resume, 56
Reduction in Force, 26, 135, 136
  alternatives, 131-133
References (employees), 77-79
References (employers), 120
Relationships (workplace),
  dynamics, 124
  maintaining, 94-96, 124-126
  types of, 125-126
Responsibility,
  taking for yourself, 153
Resumes (employees),
  action verbs, 55-56
  assessment, 29-30, 53, 142
  degrees, 48-49
  disabilities, 154-155
  dumbing down, 46-47
  employer preference, 35-37
  format, 35-37
  future-directed, 40-42, 53-56, 67-68, 145-146
  gaps in employment, 43-45
  human resources, 50-52
  networking, 65, 66, 70
  phrases for, 55
  quantitative info. in, 56
  samples, 38-39
  updating, 62, 102
Resume (employers), 113-114
Retention,
  of employees, 127-130

Role models,
  in workshops, 157

S

Salary ranges, 80-81
Saratoga Institute, *Why Employees Leave*, 127
Self-image (see image)
  positive, 20
Severance, 131, 133, 136,
Sexual harassment, 97-99
Statement of objectives, 40, 43
  samples, 41
Supervisors,
  difficult, 88-91

T

Technology firms, 127, 128

V

Visualizing,
  for success, 19-23, 29, 61, 63, 142
  your experience, 44
Virginia's Center for Innovative Technology,
  cost of replacing an employee, 127-128

W

Workplace,
  leadership in, 149
  success in, 102-105, 150
  today's environment, 149

MORRIS • ASSOCIATES, INC.
A LINCOLNSHIRE INTERNATIONAL PARTNER

Outplacement • Coaching • Training & Development

Morris Associates, Inc. takes pride in providing services and programs in the field of career development, tailored to meet the specific needs of organizations and employees. A sampling of our services is listed below. Contact us for an expanded service list and to discuss how we can customize programs for you or your organization.

OUTPLACEMENT & CAREER TRANSITION:
- Career Development
- Organizational Downsizing — Planning & Implementation
- Individual Outplacement for Professionals, Executives & Staff
- Group Outplacement & Corporate Transition Centers

EXECUTIVE & MANAGEMENT COACHING:
- Individual Career Development
- Performance-Improvement Coaching
- Group Coaching — Strengthening Managers & Supervisors

SKILLS DEVELOPMENT WORKSHOPS & SEMINARS:
- Behavior-Based Interviewing
- Career Assessment
- Marketing Yourself after 50: Good News for Gray Hairs
- Coaching & Counseling for Managers & Supervisors
- Conflict Resolution & Interpersonal Communication
- E-mail Etiquette
- Using Emotional Intelligence to Lead
- Leading, Managing & Coping with Change
- Performance Management & Evaluation
- Planning & Conducting Productive Meetings
- Resumes from the Reader's Point of View
- Time Management
- Writing, Editing & Proofreading

FACILITATION OF RETREATS & BUSINESS MEETINGS:
- Conference Planning & Meeting Management
- Team Building . . . Problem Solving . . . Project Productivity

1000 Connecticut Avenue, NW Suite 1200
Washington, DC 20036-5326
Phone: (202) 835-1750 Fax: (202) 835-1751
www.morrisdc.com

About The Author

Thomas W. Morris III, CMF, president of Morris Associates, Inc., has coached thousands of individuals going through career development and transitions, and has consulted with hundreds of firms and organizations experiencing change and reorganization. For 25 years, he has successfully worked in the private, government and non-profit sectors coaching managers, executives and professionals engaged in career development and transition.

He is certified as a Career Management Fellow. He is a past president of the Washington Area Chapter of the Association of Career Professionals International, and for two years he was a member of the Board of Governors of the International Board for Career Management Certification.

He has served on more than 20 leadership boards, committees and advisory groups including Job Connection, a job fair for people with disabilities that over five years involved more than 100 employers and over 2000 participants.

A sought-after speaker and writer, Tom has written or been quoted in articles for local and national websites, newspapers and magazines including CareerBuilder.com, RCJobs.com, WashingtonPost.com, *The Washington Post*, the *Los Angeles Times*, *National Business Employment Weekly*, *Career Planning and Adult Development Journal*, *The Riley Guide*, *Personnel*, *Mademoiselle*, *IT Recruiter*, *Washingtonian* and *Executive Update*.

Contact Us

We would like your feedback. Please tell us what you think, and whether or not this book has been helpful to you.

Contact us at:

>Morris Associates, Inc.
>1000 Connecticut Avenue, NW
>Suite #1200
>Washington, DC 20036
>
>Phone (202) 835-1750
>Fax   (202) 835-1751
>
>E-mail: mai@morrisdc.com
>
>Log onto www.morrisdc.com to learn more about our services.
>
>To order copies of this book, please call us at (202) 835-1750, or e-mail us at mai@morrisdc.com. You may also contact our distributor — Bramor Distributing at (202) 331-7231 or e-mail at bramordistributing@yaoo.com.